SEAMOUNT

D1009343

Bill Brubaker

ISBN-13: 978-1530335718

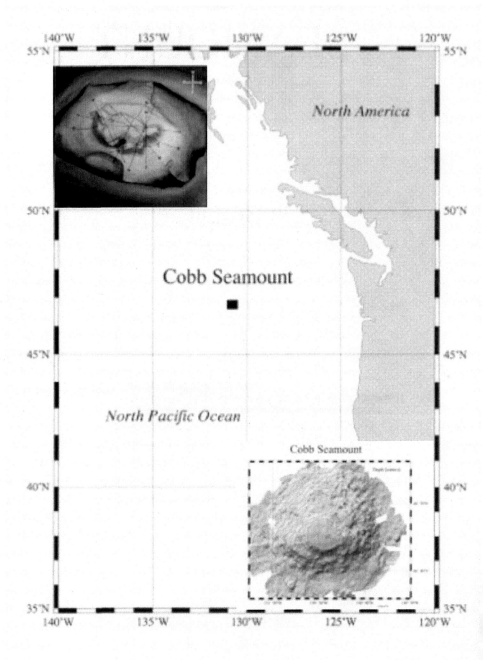

140°W   135°W   130°W   125°W   120°W

North America

Cobb Seamount

■

North Pacific Ocean

Cobb Seamount

"…man must first unlock the scientific secrets of the oceans before he can open the door to their utilization."

Daniel J. Evans,
Governor
Washington State
1965 - 1977

DEDICATION

Dedicated to the men and women of Project Sea-Use who, with courage and passion and little money dared to explore the unknown. And whether they knew it or not significantly advanced the science of oceanography and ocean engineering.

CONTENTS

FORWARD

The nine "Project Sea-Use exploratory missions to the Cobb Seamount can be described as among great lifetime adventures. Bill Brubaker's Book "Seamount" is a well written documentary of an ambitious undersea project to explore and utilize the oceans.

At a time when astronauts and space explorations had captured the nation's spirit of adventure, a small group of agencies and private ventures focused their attention and efforts on making a footprint in undersea exploration. Bill describes the character of the people and the agencies that formulated the plan to explore and inhabit the Cobb Seamount, a ten thousand foot mountain that lies off the Washington State Coast in the North Pacific Ocean.

Bill's account takes the reader on the missions to the undersea mountain and on mission dives with the Sea-Use dive teams. Bill chronicles the successes and failures of the mission objectives and shares insight into the character of the shipboard personnel supporting the mission and the divers who carried out the exploration and undersea tasks. I trust the reader will find this book a very thorough and interesting account of a very fascinating ocean exploration project.

Bill is the right person to write this account as he was a valued member of the Project Sea-Use team.

Spence Campbell
Diving Supervisor
Project Sea-Use

Author's Note:

In 1962 Spence Campbell completed a 557 mile swim of the Clearwater, Snake and Columbia Rivers, the river route of explorers Lewis & Clark, the details of which are in his book Lewis And Clark and Me. In his second book After The Swim, Campbell writes of his experiences exploring the Cobb Seamount.

INTRODUCTION

Twenty-seven million years ago on an abyssal plain West of what is today the Pacific Northwest Coast, there was a towering mountain ten thousand feet high. There were no men to climb this mountain and about the only life one could imagine, might have been some pre-historic animals that found food and shelter at its base. In time this majestic "peak" gave way to the sea...only to be discovered in the twentieth century.

Unlike the founding of new worlds and great lands, discovery of what is known today as the Cobb Seamount was somewhat uneventful and would have gone unnoticed had it not been for the curiosity and persistence of the crew of a small fisheries research vessel named the John N. Cobb. And had it not been for the fact this ten thousand foot high prehistoric mountain rose to within 130 feet of the surface, the Cobb Seamount, might have been relegated to navigational charts as just another of over a hundred under-water mountains that dot the edge of the Cascadia Basin, the mammoth void which separates the Pacific Northwest from the abyssal plain beyond.

As the crew of the John N. Cobb had proved when they discovered the Seamount, it could be approached from the surface. And the fact it could be studied unfettered by the geologic vagaries of a continental coastline did not escape the scientists.

Within two years of its discovery, the Cobb Seamount became an under water laboratory as scientists, oceanologists, indeed people of all scientific disciplines and persuasions began probing, exploring and recording the wealth of data found on the mountain's pinnacle. By 1956 scientists from the University of Washington, who by then had made three trips to the Cobb Seamount, were able to provide a reasonable description of the mountain's summit:

> "It is a relatively flat area, oval in shape and covering an area of about twenty acres. The pinnacle is in three terraces, the lowest of which is about three-thousand feet below the surface and about eight acres in diameter."

Mostly because of limited technology, early explorations of the Cobb Seamount involved the lowering of unmanned instrument packages from ships on the surface. It wasn't until 1965 that scientists descended to the mountaintop to see for themselves the potential of this great underwater laboratory. With underwater television and photography, and first-hand reports from divers, the Cobb Seamount became something more than a scientific oddity, but an oceanographic super-star. Scientists realized, for the first time perhaps, that a Seamount the top of which was barely under the surface, could become a base for environmental monitoring and deep ocean engineering technology. But it wasn't until fifteen years after its discovery that the technology to adequately explore the Cobb Seamount was developed and it was almost too late.

By then the United States had its mountain to climb... space! The exploration of space turned the money and the attention of the nation skyward and despite the pleas of a dedicated few that the oceans held an answer to the world's future food and energy needs, astronauts not aquanauts became the heroes of the day. Because there was no "national" commitment to "inner" space, to which the oceans were often referred, it was largely left to local governments, universities and private industry to explore the vast untapped wealth of the world's oceans.

In 1966, the Washington State Oceanographic Commission was established by the State Legislature to undertake a regional effort of ocean exploration using the Cobb Seamount as its focal point. Supported by the resources and technology provided by the University of Washington, Battelle Northwest Laboratories, Honeywell Marine Systems and the States of Washington, Oregon and Alaska, the Commission initiated an ambitious plan that would demonstrate that a region, the Pacific Northwest, could organize and execute a scientific and engineering program. One that would utilize a regional resource, develop a capacity to study and evaluate the usefulness of the Cobb Seamount, and by using ocean engineering technology, demonstrate that man could perform meaningful work and underwater construction on a Seamount reasonably distant from land.

In 1968, with funding from the states and limited donations from private industry, "Project Sea-Use" began.

CHAPTER 1

discovery

The discovery of the Cobb Seamount was more of a "happy accident" than the result of great scientific endeavor. The discoverers, Captain Sheldon Johnson and US Fish and Wildlife scientist Donald Powell, had no thought of making such a significant discovery when, in June of 1950, they left Seattle for a summer of exploratory fishing. Their intention was to track the runs of tuna and other species of fish as the fish migrated along the Washington Coast and by doing so, give commercial fishermen better information on when, where and how to catch fish. The emphasis, it seemed was on the "how" since the vessel on which they sailed was owned and operated by the US Fish and Wildlife's Gear Development Division.

On this trip most of the scientific "stuff" was left to Powell, since Captain Johnson was more concerned with breaking in a new boat...his first new boat in more than thirty years at sea.

The boat was called the John N. Cobb, named in honor of the founder of University of Washington's College of Fisheries. It was launched from Tacoma Washington's Western Boat Building Company just six months prior to departing Seattle on the trip now underway.

The general design of the boat was that of a purse seiner, but modified to allow a variety of fishing services. After all the Cobb was a fisheries research vessel. The wheelhouse and machinery spaces were further aft than that of a traditional purse seiner and the stern was elliptical rather than flat and broad, characteristic of conventional purse seiners.

The 83 foot-long hull was literally crammed with the most modern navigation and scientific equipment available, including a new device called LORAN; Long Range Radio Navigation. With LORAN Captain Johnson could pinpoint to the nearest yard, the ships exact location at sea, While that was important for scientific reports, after thirty years at sea, Captain Johnson had a pretty good idea where he was at any time.

Most of the equipment aboard the little boat was, however, there to support the ship's mission of exploratory fishing. A Fathometer could give scientists an immediate graphic and numeric readings on the depth of water below. Information from the Bendix Echo-sounder allowed the scientists to tell what, if anything was below the ship. There were devices to measure the temperature of

13

the water, take samples from the bottom and a small laboratory equipped with holding tanks for any specimens taken from the ocean.

On deck, the variety of fishing gear would confuse the best of those who take pride in identifying the many and varied types of fishing vessels of the Pacific Northwest Coast. Poles from which long-lines were attached identified the Cobb as a West Coast Troller. But the small launch with the huge net-hoist on its deck gave, at quick glance, the Cobb the appearance of a Seiner. Trawling gear aboard the ship was even more confusing to the uninitiated. The Cobb, it would seem was truly a "maritime jack-of-all trades"

In addition to her deck hands, of which there were usually eight, the Cobb normally carried three scientists. But on this occasion there was only one scientist in addition to the crew…that was Don Powell.

On Sunday July 23rd, 1950, the Cobb was slowly making her way through choppy seas on a Northerly course from Astoria, Oregon headed to Alaska. Except for a stop at Astoria for fuel and water, the Cobb had been at sea since June. The nets, with which Captain Johnson hoped to sample a fish run or two, had been deployed about an hour, but so far…nothing! The day before the nets had produced only one tuna and five small sharks. It was readily apparent the sharks had made short work of any run of tuna in the area.

The morning sun had been up over an hour already when Johnson and Powell sighted an unusual number of sea-birds dead ahead, unusual because they were well over two-hundred miles from the coast where sea-birds are more likely to find food on or near the surface. Not knowing what was causing the birds to congregate Johnson hauled in the nets as a precaution and proceeded toward the birds. Such a gathering of sea-birds usually meant food and that meant fish. Not only did Johnson and Powell wonder what the birds were doing so far from shore, as they could detect no warm water up-welling associated with a surface food supply.

As Captain Johnson kept the little "jack-of-all-trades" fishing boat on course toward the birds, Powell turned on the Fathometer. The instrument would tell them how deep the water is beneath the ship. Neither Powell nor the Captain were worried, at over two hundred miles from shore there was not much danger of hitting bottom. In fact the pair didn't expect the Fathometer to even read the bottom depth. It would, however, tell them if there were a school of fish beneath them.

The initial readings put the depth at five hundred fathoms, nearly three thousand feet. Powell thought it strange that he would get any readings at all since the charts showed the bottom in excess of twelve thousand feet. As Powell watched, the depth readings began to decrease...four hundred fathoms...three hundred... two then one hundred fathoms. It could be a school of fish, Powell thought, tuna most likely, but he wasn't sure. Tuna run in tight compact swarms, often giving the appearance on the instruments of a solid object. On more than one occasion fishing boats like the Cobb have located submarines on their instruments not knowing for sure it was a school of fish or not.

As the Cobb steamed forward, the Fathometer continued to read out fewer fathoms. Powell flipped on the Echo-depth sounder, a sort of vertical radar which would give them a better visual representation of what was below. If it were a school of fish the depth-sounder would tell them as the machine read out contours much like a topographic map used in surveying land. The instrument recorded bottom at twenty fathoms then began to read deeper. Whatever it was the Cobb had passed over it. There was now little doubt to the two of them that it was bottom, not a school of fish they were seeing, but what?. They were over two hundred miles from land.

Johnson wheeled the little craft about for another pass and as before the instruments began to read shallower. If in fact it was bottom they were seeing then it had to be some sort of underwater mountain, a seamount. But the charts showed nothing. How could one of these huge pre-historic mountains gone undiscovered for so long, Johnson wondered? The charts showed a line of seamounts along the Northwest Coastline. Captan Johnson often took great delight in navigating this string of underwater mountains with colorful names like Bear, Thompson, Heck and Explorer Seamounts. It stood to reason that whatever was below them, was probably a forgotten or yet discovered "peak" in an ancient mountain range.

After several passes over the "summit", Johnson and Powell were convinced and made the following entry into the ship's log.... Then in red pencil, Captain Johnson wrote.....

Latitude 46 degrees, 44 minutes North

Longitude 130 degrees, 47 minutes West

Then Captain Johnson wrote.....

"Discovered Seamount"

There was no jumping up or down, or wild expression of joy. After all they were scientists and discovery was what they were trained to do. Yet deep down both Powell and Johnson felt a "rush" of excitement thinking they had found something of significance that no one else had found. And yes, the thought had crossed the Captain's mind that a newly discovered seamount would have to have a name. The Johnson Seamount, he thought to himself, had a nice ring to it! While Johnson dreamed, if only for a moment that the seamount would be named for him, his superiors believed it was more appropriate to name the newly discovered underwater mountain for the ship that found it so as not to discredit others who had a hand in its discovery. It would be named The Cobb Seamount.

Confirming the discovery, whether by the best scientific means or in his own experienced mind, did little to ease Captain Johnson's concern however that something might be sticking up out of the water or just under the surface. It was a big ocean and likely a big seamount and highly unlikely that in a few passes they could or would have sailed over all of it.

For the next three hours the crew of the intrepid little fishing boat passed back and forth over the seamount. Each time Johnson would steer the ship in one direction until the Fathometer read four hundred fathoms or more, then turn the ship back and go the other way until the Fathometer again read four hundred fathoms or more. He repeated this procedure until he had covered and charted the peak below. The resulting grid measured four by eight miles. Both Johnson and Powell were convinced that what was below them was bottom and not a school of tuna. But to make sure, as any good scientist would do, they ordered the crew to set two long lines of halibut gear at seventy fathoms. Then as before, he passed over the pinnacle several times in several directions. When the lines were hauled in after about an hour they had caught not halibut, but bottom fish…four hundred and fifty pounds of Red Snapper and Rock Sole. They were big fish too, which meant a bountiful food supply not to far below the surface.

As a matter of routine, Captain Johnson would report to the Fish and Wildlife Service office in Seattle twice a day, at the same time each day. He would give whomever answered the radio information on their location, the weather, fish runs and any other information that might be of interest or use to the fishing fleets that plied the waters off the coasts of Washington, Oregon and Alaska. Discovery of a seamount, it seemed would be information of interest, but Johnson felt no need to break the schedule and rejected Powell's urgings to phone home. Reports of seamount discoveries were not uncommon and ships at sea would often report to the U-S Coast and Geodetic Survey a discovery of a seamount only to find it was a school of fish. The resulting razzing did little for one's scientific credibility…or ego for that matter. Whatever the reason, Captain Johnson, never-the-less convinced he had discovered a seamount and not a school of fish, set course for Alaska and left the "Johnson" Seamount behind.

Joe Ellison, Captain Johnson's immediate supervisor at the Fish and Wildlife Service was closest to the radio when Johnson made his first scheduled report of the day. Johnson casually mentioned that he had some news in addition to his regular report, but proceeded to give his reports first. The seas, he said, were moderate with swells eight to twelve feet. It was slightly overcast and there was a four knot wind from the Northeast. No tuna yet, but they may be found farther north, he told Ellison over the radio.

After the report and the usual exchange of pleasantries Ellison asked Johnson what the "news" was. "We've discovered a seamount," came the reply.

"It's a big one," he added and gave the home base the exact coordinates. The more Johnson described his discovery, the more excited he got, but that excitement, it appeared, wasn't shared by Ellison or the others in the office that had, by now, gathered around the radio. "My guess," Johnson continued, "is that it's a mountain ten to twelve thousand feet high with a relatively flat top four by eight miles across. The amazing thing," Johnson said, "is that its top is less than two hundred feet from the surface...over!"

The pause on the other end of the radio transmission was understandable. From what Captain Johnson described, it was highly unlikely that it was anything but what he said it was. But Ellison's charts didn't show anything at 46 degrees, 44 minutes North - 130 degrees, 47 minutes West. Nothing! As Johnson and Powell huddled around the radio set in the Cobb's small pilot house, Ellison pressed his questions, repeatedly noting that there was nothing on his charts to indicate that what Johnson and Powell had discovered was a seamount. "We're sure," Johnson repeated. "it's no school of fish, its no submarine and it ain't no whale...

it's a   seamount and I know it's a seamount because I anchored on it!"

Later that day, after the Cobb had departed the vicinity of the newly discovered seamount and began making its way to Alaska, Fish and Wildlife in Seattle radioed that the U-S Coast and Geodetic Survey was very interested in Johnson's discovery and wanted more information, which he was directed to immediately provide on his return from Alaska.

On September 14th, 1950, The Cobb was back on station above the seamount. Immediately Johnson and Powell began to recheck all the data they had obtained during their first survey of the underwater mountain. Using the depth finder and the echo-sounder, they repeated the tedious, but necessary crisscrossing of the pinnacle in order to confirm what they already tested and what they already knew. The electronic gear was accurate, no doubt, but Don Powell was a belt and suspenders kind of guy, and just to make sure he suggested to Captain Johnson that they "throw the lead" to determine the depth to the mountain's top. The "lead" in this case was in fact a led ball about the size of softball attached to a line marked off in fathoms. It was used by both ancient and modern day mariners to determine the depth of shallow water. Both Johnson and Powell were surprised that after only a couple of throws, they found the mountain's top to be only 130 feet below the surface, much closer than they had thought or the electronic gear had indicated.

Their next step was to rig a mechanical bottom sampler, a small clamshell device that would scoop up a portion of the bottom and bring it to the surface. First attempts proved only an exercise as there was nothing in the sampler when it was brought to the surface. The results were better when they moved to deeper water where they recovered a variety of rocks, gravel and soil mixed with an abundance of small marine organisms. Sample after sample was brought up, bottled and labeled, until finally the sea, as it always seems to do, claimed the sampler which had apparently snagged on a rock on the pinnacle's surface. Left on the seamount, in addition to the bottom sampler were several units of fishing gear, two long lines and one net...so noted in the log book as a warning to anyone who might follow, that operating in relatively shallow water in the open ocean had its perils.

Undaunted by the loss of the bottom sampler, Powell again resorted to ancient marine technique to solve his problem of retrieving samples from the bottom. Using a leaded line, Powell attached a mass of tallow or wax to its end. The idea was for the soft, sticky tallow to pick up loose debris on the pinnacle. While a more tedious process, it worked and the crew was able to finish the task.

For three days the Cobb remained on station, sometimes anchored, other times steaming to different points above the four by eight mile plateau. Each time Captain Johnson extended his fishing gear and each time retrieved large amount of bottom fish.

On September 16, the John N. Cobb, her holds filled with fish and her labs stuffed with samples for Fish & Wildlife and the Coast & Geodetic Survey, turned about and headed for home. Captain Johnson was informed by his office that the Seattle Newspapers had gotten word of the discovery and published an article before the "higher ups" had a chance to be informed. The Fish and Wildlife folks were a bit upset by that but Johnson reminded them that the radio channels used by the service are public and that a lot of people, even newspaper people listen to them.

By discovery, the Cobb Seamount became a focal point of scientific research. Unlike other nearby seamounts, the Cobb Seamount rose to within 130 feet of the ocean's surface, thus opening the way for many types of scientific exploration. But that wouldn't come for yet another decade after Captain Johnson's historic discovery. For more immediate purposes, the Cobb Seamount provided a ready made platform for the stationing of scientific instruments with which to study the ocean, its movements and its inhabitants, far off the coast of Northwest America. Intrigued by the accounts of Cobb's discovery, scientists throughout the nation, but primarily the University of Washington in Seattle, began to make plans for its use.

CHAPTER 2

early utilization

The Cobb Seamount was, for the University of Washington, a natural, ready made laboratory in the University's own back yard. Using the Cobb Seamount would only enhance the University's Oceanography School, which was already known for its leadership in the study of marine sciences.

Between 1952 and 1954, The University of Washington made nine trips to the Cobb Seamount, all of them for the purpose of surveying the underwater mountain. All of the surveillance during this time was done from the surface. It wasn't until April of 1961 that the first instrument "package" was actually lowered to the pinnacle. The "package", which was designed by advance oceanography students at the University, contained a flow meter to measure the currents that passed over the pinnacle. It was lowered to the plateau from the University's research vessel "Brown Bear".

The instrument "package" remained on the pinnacle for four days, then was retrieved by the students and returned to the University. The data collected bore out the observations of Sheldon Johnson and Don Powell just over two years before, that there were strong currents that passed over the pinnacle. These currents, the scientists noted, were not unlike the winds that can blow across the top of a "regular" mountain…like Washington's Mount Rainier. The fact these currents carried an abundant food supply would account for the large numbers of fish.

More detailed surveys of the Seamount were made in the summers of 1963, 64 and 1967. The purpose of these surveys was more geologic in nature since an underlying premise of the scientists at the University and Coast and Geodetic Survey was that the Cobb Seamount would be an ideal location for the establishment of permanent instrument packages. The University of Washington Scientists learned from their previous trips that waiting on the surface while the instruments did their thing was, at best, a waste of valuable scientific time. And there was always the question of weather. Trying to remain on-station during a storm, even when anchored, left a lot to be desired.

One thing upon which oceanologist agreed was measurement of the "interface, that point where the oceans and atmosphere meet, was made more difficult if not less accurate because the measurements had to be made from instruments that were either floating on the surface or flying in the atmosphere. Simply put, the instruments became part of the environment and therefore were subject to the movements of each. The Cobb Seamount was seen as an ideal location for the establishment of a permanent structure that was located in the ocean but not part of it, and far enough away as to not be affected by the coastline.

The possibilities of using the Cobb Seamount for scientific endeavors were, it seemed, limitless and set inquiring minds into high gear. Meteorologist saw the Cobb as an ideal site to erect a mast with which to study and measure the weather…away from the interference of other natural forces. Biologist and environmentalist were quick to point out that before anything is attached to the mountaintop, scientists must examine the surface of the mountain before it is disturbed. Of particular interest was a comparative analysis of underwater flora and fauna on the mountain and on bottom much closer to the land mass.

Then there were the geologists who were convinced the Cobb Seamount offered a unique opportunity to study the sea floor and learn more about the structural history of the Northeast Pacific Ocean.

But to allow these fairly diverse scientific disciplines to "run amuck" on the Cobb would serve no scientific purpose. The scientific assaults on the mountain had to be carefully planned, coordinated and carried out in an orderly fashion. To accomplish this, the University of Washington Departments of Oceanography, Atmospheric Sciences, the Applied Physics Laboratory and ESSA, the Federal Environmental Agency, joined forces to create an interdepartmental program for the utilization and detailed study of the Cobb Seamount and the surrounding area.

In 1963 The University's Applied Physics Laboratory placed two instruments on the pinnacle. The instruments, a temperature sensor and a current or flow meter, were not unlike the instruments placed there two years before by advanced students.

Until 1965 all experiments, including the APL's two-week project, were conducted from the surface. What scientists and explorers desperately wanted was some first-hand accounts of what it was like on the top of the ten thousand foot underwater mountain. It was no trick to send a diver to a depth of 130 feet. In fact divers had descended far deeper. Most, if not all of these deep dives, had been accomplished in relatively protected water, not in the open ocean hundreds of miles from shore and off the continental shelf. The problem was not so much one for the divers, but for the support ships that had to maintain station above them. Giant swells and currents, not to mention sudden storms could sweep the divers life support out of reach in a matter of minutes.

In the Summer of 1965, eighteen scientists and divers boarded the University of Washington Research Vessel "Brown Bear" for the 40 hour trip to the Cobb Seamount. The expedition leader was Walter Sands, Senior Oceanographer at the University. Sands believed that after a detailed study of the pinnacle, a permanent structure of some sort could be erected there. Sands had in mind A 150-foot tower, thirty to forty feet of which would rise above the surface. The tower, he declared, would be like a radio tower and could support instruments both above and below the surface and transmit information back to the mainland. This, he believed, would solve any problems caused by the inter-face, where the ocean and the atmosphere meet. The instruments on the tower would be in the environment they were to measure, but not part of it. Therefor the data collected would, he believed, be more accurate than data collected from measuring devices subject to the natural movement of the wind and waves.

The 1965 expedition was the first major effort to explore the Cobb Seamount since its discovery fifteen years before. It was financed by the National Science Foundation and the Office Of Naval Research. Other participating agencies included the Boeing Airplane Company of Seattle and Ocean Systems Incorporated, a marine engineering firm headed by Jon Lindbergh, son of aviator Charles Lindbergh. In May of that year, five divers from the Brown Bear expedition descended to the summit of the Seamount for the first ever "in-person" look. Because of the difficulty of anchoring the ship above the mountain, the divers operated from small rubber boats called Zodiac Boats a safe distance from the Brown Bear. This allowed the divers to operate free of any danger from the ship's propellers that were always turning in order to keep it on station.

For Ron Ririe, Russell Sweetland, Joseph Staley, Dale Kisker and Robert Williams, their "tour" of the Seamount would, of necessity, be short. Using compressed air and SCUBA gear, their effective time at depth without decompressing on the way up, was about ten minutes, hardly enough time to do anything more than snap a few pictures and get a sense of what the pinnacle was like. The trade-off however, was the freedom with which they were able to conduct their business, unencumbered by surface supplied air which, because of the hoses, limits the amount of movement.

With the assistance of five "back-up" divers, more than nine total hours were spent on the Cobb Seamount proving to Sands, at least, that divers using SCUBA devices could do useful work on the open ocean floor even though it was only 130 feet deep.

The notion of divers doing useful work on the ocean floor was nothing new. In the early sixties the United States Navy embarked on a ambitious program called "Man In The Sea" which sought to prove that human beings could work at depths up to a thousand feet. The program was characterized by three successive projects entitled Sea-lab 1, ll, and lll. In two of the Sea-lab experiments, divers operated from habitats placed on the ocean floor. The third Sea-lab, while planned, never came to pass primarily because the fledgling U-S Space Program was drawing attention and money away from any efforts to probe the world's oceans.

While divers were exploring the Cobb Seamount, engineers from the Boeing Airplane Company were topside proving that Sand's vision of a 150-foot tower permanently located on the Seamount wasn't such a bad idea after-all.

The Boeing Company had been experimenting with "meteor-burst communications since 1958. Until now, the idea of bouncing radio signals off the trails of falling stars was mostly theory. During World War Two, radar operators would often get false signals which they attributed to reflections from the ionized trails of meteorites that enter the earth's atmosphere by the millions. And even though the meteor trails lasted only seconds, using them to transmit data provided greater signal stability and control than could be obtained in conventional radio transmission. Boeing had established an experimental link between Seattle and Bozeman, Montana in 1959 using a system developed by the company's antsubmarine warfare division. It was mostly a research project with little   utilitarian value at the time. According to Boeing's ASW Systems Manager Paul Pflueger, the 1965 Cobb Seamount mission provided a wonderful opportunity to test the system using data actually obtained by scientists on station. For the first time oceanographic information was sent via meteor-burst to the Inglewood Research Station near Issaquah, Washington. Both Sands and Pflueger were elated and figured that by using a land based master control system, they could send a signal skyward and find a meteor trail at the proper angle to the ocean base station. The reflected signal would then tell the ocean-based equipment to release stored data which would be sent back to the earth station via the same meteor trail. It was all very space age, but it worked.

The idea of erecting an instrument mast or tower on the Cobb Seamount wasn't, as it turned out, exclusively the genius of Walter Sands. Scientists and engineers at Oregon State University had been watching closely the "goings-on"" at Cobb with an eye, no doubt, on cashing in on the scientific potential of an accessible underwater mountain. As Sands and his divers were scouring the Cobb's pinnacle, OSU Oceanographer Jim Washburn was putting to paper a design for a 180 foot mast that he hoped would eventually be placed on the Seamount...before anyone else.

The structure, called Totem 1, was launched in September of 1967, but instead of going directly to the Cobb, it was erected in protected water off the Oregon Coast in order to test the integrity of the mooring system. Washburn knew it was the mooring system that was the key to successfully placing any structure on Cobb. The mooring system passed with flying colors and work then began in building another tower to be called Totem II, which would be placed on the pinnacle.

In June of 1968 two research vessels, left Newport, Oregon for the Cobb Seamount. Towed behind one of them, looking more like a big log than a scientific instrument, was Totem II, the

178 foot long, 42 inch diameter tower that Walter Sands longed to place there first. The new mast or tower differed from Totem I in that the floatable tanks used to stabilize the mast in heavy swells, were eliminated and the Totem II was strengthened to withstand the tensions of anchor cables. At one end of the mast was a six-foot "spud" that would simply sit on the mountaintop. Four submerged anchors would hold the mast in place. It was called a "hard moor" whereby the wave and surge forces on the mast would be passed directly to wire cables which were attached to a fairlead about halfway up the mast at one end and to the anchors at the other. Just above where the upper mooring cables were attached to the Totem, was an instrument house that contained a complete automated weather station that Washburn was able to get on loan from the Navy's Research Laboratory. Above the instrument house was a hoist for moving equipment on and off the tower. The plan was to attach two of the anchors to the Totem's fairleads, then flood the lower half of the spar while pressurizing the upper half. If there were no hang-ups, Totem II would simply rotate to a vertical position and be lowered to the surface of the Seamount. The anchors would then be manipulated into position using lines from the two ships then the entire assembly would be guided into position on the mountain.

It seemed so simple on paper.

As the scientists and crew members began to pressurize the upper portion of Totem they discovered a crack in the stem, probably the result of stress while being towed nearly three hundred miles. Since the crack was above the waterline it could be repaired, but by now the lower half had been submerged and there was no way to test the integrity of the stem below water. Washburn could only hope.

The operation continued however and the two anchors and the tower were put in place...but not without one very tense moment. During the process two members of Washburn's team were on the mast. As they sought to stabilize the half submerged structure, the Totem was over trimmed and the two scientist-divers found themselves "riding" the Totem as if it were a rodeo horse. They were not hurt, just shaken a bit by the ride.

The next day a third anchor was set, but a fourth anchor proved to be a problem. It eventually sank in an estimated three thousand feet of water and was lost. In its place the team rigged a three thousand-pound Danforth Anchor and by weeks end Totem II was ready, or so it seemed. Washburn and his team had hoped to erect the mast in rather quick fashion once the anchors were in place. However it took an entire day just to tighten and tension the cables between the anchors and the fairlead attachment points on the Totem. It was finally done and now time to place instruments on the mast, the very reason for the mast.

No sooner had work begun on installing the instruments, work was halted when divers reported there was a large dent in the lower stem about 33 feet from the bottom. Washburn ordered all personnel off the Totem then sent divers down for a closer look. The divers reported back that a compression failure had occurred during the erection process. It was clear to Washburn and the others that to re-float the Totem, and tow it back to Newport for repairs was out of the question. The structure, Washburn surmised, would not survive another three hundred-mile voyage. The decision was to leave Totem II in place, remove all the instruments except for a light and a fog horn, and return to Newport and construct a sleeve to be placed over the dented portion as a reinforcement. Before they could do that, Totem II broke in half. A portion of the mast was found floating above the Seamount when Washburn returned in July. He managed to retrieve what he could of the Totem in hopes of repairing it and returning to the Cobb Seamount. A year later Washburn did return to the Cobb, but not with a "fixed up" Totem II, but as part of a far more ambitious program to explore the underwater mountain.

CHAPTER 3

project sea-use

As demonstrated by the 1965 expedition and the ill-fated Oregon State University adventure, interest in the Cobb Seamount continued to build. In 1968 a multi-year, multi-million dollar program for further exploration and eventual use of the seamount began. The program, called "Project Sea-Use," had among its goals the placement of scientific instruments on the Seamount with which to gather scientific data with the ultimate objective to establishing a manned habitat on the pinnacle. The habitat would provide scientists, engineers and divers a permanent facility from which scientific and engineering experiments could be conducted. The habitat, as envisioned, would not be unlike those used in the U-S Navy's SEALAB project that was designed to test the feasibility of long term living and working underwater.

Just as important a goal of Project Sea-Use was to demonstrate that a region, in this case the Pacific Northwest, could initiate, organize and execute a scientific project using regional resources with participation from both the public and private sectors as well as educational institutions.

The sponsor of Project Sea-Use was the Washington State Oceanographic Commission, a body of elected legislators, citizens, businessman and scientists, whose charter was to oversee the State of Washington's participation in any actives that had to do with the ocean's resources. Fishing, off-shore oil exploration and transport and scientific study of the marine environment were the primary impetus for the Commission's formation. The Washington State Legislature, which created the Commission, did so with the idea of enhancing the State's position as a center for oceanographic activity. A retired Navy Admiral, Emory Stanley Junior, volunteered to be the Project Sea-Use manager and as the Navy's former Auditor General was well qualified to run an under-funded program like Sea-Use. Admiral Stanley thought of the Cobb Seamount as a national underseas laboratory where scientists and technicians could work in the areas of interest to them. "It is," he stated, "a resource not duplicated in any other region of the United States." As such Admiral Stanley entertained the notion of designating the Cobb Seamount as the first National Seamount Station.

By its discovery, the Cobb Seamount was a "target of opportunity" and soon became the primary objective of the Commission's attention. Because the Commission could do little more than make policy, the actual management of the program became the responsibility of the Oceanographic Institute of Washington. The Institute or OIW, as it was known, was created by the Oceanographic Commission as a planning agency to develop program sponsors, solicit participation from various private and public agencies and most important raise the money necessary to carry out the program. The Institute in turn delegated over-all authority to the sponsor representatives who became the Sea-Use Council, a regional forum of agencies tasked with coordinating the scientific exploration of the Seamount on behalf of its members. In addition to the Institute, government agencies participating in the project included ESSA, the Environmental Science Services Administration and the Bureau of Commercial Fisheries.

Participating educational institutions include the Universities of Washington, Oregon, Alaska and Hawaii, plus Western Washington State College and the Virginia Mason Research Center in Seattle. No endeavor of this magnitude would be accomplished without the involvement of private industry. The firms of Honeywell, The NERUS Corporation, Murphy-Pacific Salvage, the NUMEC Company and Westinghouse were urged to join the project. The "meeting place" for these participants was the Sea-Use Council which added to its ranks the United States Navy and Coast Guard, The Maritime Administration, and the British Columbia Ministries of Environment and Public Lands. The Sea-Use Council was chaired by Admiral Stanley who immediately formed a unit within the Council that would administer the Sea-Use funds. Admiral Stanley selected another Navy man to head that unit; retired Commander Charles Gott. The Sea-Use Program was to also include the news media whose representatives were asked to become members of yet another sub-set of the Oceanographic Institute Of Washington called the Sea-Use Committee.

When the Sea-Use project became a Regional-State-Federal and Provincial effort, the emphasis on exploration and utilization of the Cobb Seamount was reaffirmed. A listing of possible tasks including environmental monitoring, scientific investigations and ocean engineering was compiled then narrowed to those tasks that could be reasonably funded and accomplished on Cobb.

In developing sponsors, the Institute's first goal was to designate the primary agencies that would provide the scientific, technical and financial base for Project Sea-Use. Overall coordination of the scientific assault on the Cobb Seamount fell to Battelle Northwest, a so-called "think tank" supported by government grants and private industry. Honeywell Marine Systems of Seattle served as consultant to Battelle Northwest and was also the industrial coordinator. Responsibility of the dive teams and their equipment was given to Ocean Foundation Systems of Hawaii. The University of Washington in Seattle was tasked with addition scientific coordination. For that, these sponsoring agencies contributed the sum of $91,000 for the first phase of the project, the budget for which was just over two million dollars.

In a document entitled *Project Sea-Use, Cobb Seamount,* the principals outlined a program of phased exploration that would be carried out over a four year period, with actual trips to the

Seamount during the summer months of each of the four years. While the initial trips would be exploratory in nature, it was expected that the final planned trip in the summer of 1971 would see the initial construction of a manned habitat on the mountain's summit. The vision rivaled that of Jules Verne in that the proposed habitat would not only be a home for scientists and divers, but would serve as the launch pad for an underwater vehicle capable of exploring the ocean to a depth of ten thousand feet or more. Failing that, a more realistic expectation was that the early phases of Project Sea-Use would result in a detailed report that would contain recommendations for future use of the Seamount…which could be a manned habitat of some sort.

No one would claim that the Sea-Use program and its participants had exclusive rights to the exploration of Cobb Seamount and it was generally understood, if not stated, that others were welcome. The expectation of Institute members was that others interested in the Cobb Seamount would either join Project Sea-Use as paying participants, or if they decided to go it alone they would, at least, coordinate their efforts with the Sea-Use program. No one ever did.

While there were no planned explorations of the Cobb Seamount beyond those already outlined in the Project Sea-Use proposals, there was always the possibility which raised the question…to whom does the seamount belong? And for that matter, who owns the Oceans? In 1964, a United Nations Conference on the world's oceans, asked world leaders to address that question. The conferees concluded that significant world features, like the oceans, belong to everyone. It was understood that to mean seamounts as well. The conferees further concluded that the use of these significant world features would be shared...much like Antarctica, where more than a dozen nations participate. As one might expect the United Nations envisioned itself as having jurisdiction over such world features.

The strategic nature of the Cobb Seamount was understood, if not spoken by those involved in the Sea-Use program. But it would serve no purpose for scientists and explorers to tout the military applications of such a conveniently located underwater platform. After all they were scientists and the last thing they wanted was to have the military take over their project. However Washington State's two very influential and powerful senators had no qualms about speaking of such strategic, military or otherwise, use of Cobb Seamount. In the Spring of 1968, the pair, while seeking congressional support for Project Sea-Use, called for..."United States occupation of the Seamount in order to deny its control by other nations." Flying in the face of the Project's policy of inviting all comers, and the UN Conference of 1964, Senator Warren Magnuson told the nation's lawmakers that it would be a "healthy precedent" for the United States to claim the Cobb until the ques-

An artists rendition of what many saw as the ultimate use of the Cobb Seamount...the establishment of a manned habitat on the Seamount's pinnacle from which divers and scientists could explore and carry out scientific projects without having to return to the surface. The structure as envisioned would also serve as the base of operations for submersibles such as the Westinghouse Deep-star 2000

tions involving ownership could be resolved. In his words," should it be occupied by another nation, it would be an important strategic loss for our country."

In the case of the Cobb Seamount, a claim on the basis of territory could not be legally made since it was located well beyond the territorial or conservation limits of the United States. While it has been widely accepted that occupation is sufficient to claim territory, there remained the question of the proposed habitat on the Seamount as being sufficient since it's occupation would be temporary.

Until 1968, Project Sea-Use was largely an academic exercise and its most immediate goal was to raise money. By then only about one hundred thousand dollars of the two million dollar project had been collected. It was, however, enough to begin buying equipment and start training divers. But with only a hundred grand in the bank, the process of obtaining equipment was as much a scavenger hunt than an economic exercise. As it turned out, in its four years Project Sea-Use while relying mostly on voluntary contributions of materials and services, collected just over $850,000, of which $50,000 was in cash.

The divers came from a variety of sources, including but not limited to local diving schools and community colleges that offered diver education and training. Additional diver training was provided by the Virginia Mason Research Center in Seattle and

Northwest Diving Institute, a private firm owned by Spence Campbell who also headed Virginia Mason's Diving Physiology Research Laboratory. Equipment for the Sea-Use project was, on the other hand, more difficult to obtain and that which wasn't brought to the program by the participants, was purchased outright or leased.

In addition to the States of Washington, Oregon and Alaska and Honeywell Marine Systems, various corporations with an interest in the sea responded to the invitation to participate. Notable among them was the Underseas Division of Westinghouse. For over a decade Westinghouse had been operating and perfecting its "Deepstar" series of manned submersibles . Following the initial phases of the Project Sea-Use expeditions, Westinghouse announced that its research submersible *Deepstar 2000* would participate in the second phase of the Project, Sea-Use ll. The announcement caused no small amount of excitement as it would, for the first time, allow non-diver qualified scientists and engineers to take a look at the Seamount, up close and personal. As part of the proposed package Westinghouse disclosed that it would schedule forty hours for the submersible's Cobb Seamount operations which meant taking two observers, plus the pilot, to the pinnacle numerous times.

Except for the Executive Director of the Oceanographic Commission and those men and women provided by academic institutions and the private sector participants, participation in Project Sea-Use was voluntary...meaning they didn't get paid. This applied mostly to the divers who, for the love of adventure, agreed to be trained and sent to Cobb Seamount. In 1967 a rather feeble attempt to get the State of Washington to come up with some kind of stipend for the members of the Oceanographic Commission failed. Six members of the Commission, which was the major force behind the planning and policy making for Project Sea-Use filed a law suit against the State of Washington. Among the defendants were the State's Budget Director and the State Treasurer. They claimed that the six, as members of the State Legislature when appointed to the Commission, were already being paid for their services. The State prevailed.

By winter of 1968 the Sea-Use divers had been selected and training got underway. It also marked the first time the Project Sea-Use divers were referred to, in the press, as "aquanauts." Doctor Dixy Lee Ray, head of Seattle's Pacific Science Center and Ocean Systems' Jon Lindbergh, suggested to the Oceanographic Commission, with Admiral Stanley's approval, that the 31 year old Spence Campbell be given the responsibility of selecting and training divers as well as coordinating the Phase 1 assault on Cobb Seamount. All of the diver candidates had to submit their diving experience and once chosen would be evaluated and Campbell would be given final say. Campbell, despite his youth, be was well qualified to lead the team of divers and scientists having himself logged more than three thousand diving hours, many of which as an Air Force Rescue Diver. In 1957 Campbell attended the Navy's Underwater Swim School in Florida then entered The Coastal School of Deep Sea Diving in Oakland, California where he trained as a commercial diver, mastering both SCUBA and hard-hat diving skills. In 1962 Campbell made headlines when he swam the Clearwater, Snake and Columbia Rivers retracing Lewis and Clark's 557 mile water rout to the Pacific Ocean, all to raise money for his education. The likable Campbell exhibited an energy and vitality that comes only with a love of his work. His experience and present position as head of the Lab at Virginia Mason Research Center and of course the respect of those who worked with him, made him the ideal man for the job of team leader. It all depended however on the approval of his boss and mentor, Doctor Merrill Spencer at Virginia Mason. Dr. Spencer approved, recognizing that with Project Sea-Use and Virginia Mason's participation provided an excellent opportunity to further the Research Lab's studies in diving physiology.

Assisting Campbell were three other experienced and well qualified divers; Carl Eurick and John Patton, both submarine medical technicians at Virginia Mason and Roland White, a submarine medical technician and student in the Scientific and Engineering Program at Bellevue Community College. White along with

Patton, was a graduate of Campbell's Northwest Diving Institute..
Carl Eurick was trained as a U.S. Navy diver.

Before the divers set one fin into the water at Cobb, all of those selected for the program were to undergo a vigorous dry-land training schedule that included practice sessions and classroom instruction. First on the agenda was the oxygen tolerance tests, necessary because of oxygen's toxic effects under extreme pressure such as might be encountered at Cobb. The test, used extensively by the U.S. Navy, would determine whether a diver was susceptible to oxygen toxicity. A decompression chamber, used by workers digging the Metro Sewage Tunnel in Seattle was used for the tests. Each of the candidate divers, including two members of the Seattle media selected for the project, were pressurized to a depth of sixty feet, then "fed" one hundred percent oxygen. If no ill-effects were noted divers would move to the next session. During actual dives on the Seamount, the plan was to have divers use a mixture of 50% oxygen and 50% nitrogen in order to lower the precent of oxygen that could be fatal under pressure. The mixture would also allow the divers longer times on station. All of the candidate divers passed. The next stop in the training were decompression drills aboard the ESSA Ship *Oceanographer* which was anchored in Seattle's Lake Union. The divers, working in pairs, carried two large SCUBA Tanks, surface supplied air hoses, buoyancy vests and weights just as if they were at the Cobb. The teams were lowered into the Lake's murky and sometimes muddy waters using a crane supported collapsible "chain stage." Once on the bottom of the Lake the divers were to swim a short distance away, then return to the submerged "stage" and signal to be hauled up to the ship. Since the drill was to simulate an emergency, timing was critical, Once on board, the divers were to shed their equipment including tanks and air hoses and get into the two-man decompression chamber on the ship's deck as fast as possible. All of the divers , including the two media representatives, passed this test as well, but not without some anxiety, since the bottom of the lake was mostly mud and within twenty feet of the surface it was pitch black.

By the close of 1968 the divers were as well trained as they could be, considering none of them had done open ocean diving before. One thing that Team Leader Campbell knew for sure was that the Sea-Use divers had to be good SCUBA divers, disciplined and in good physical condition. He knew what he was talking about as he had by now been a commercial diver almost three years and a great deal more experience than any of the divers selected for the assault on Cobb Seamount. The Sea-Use Phase 1 team was, in Campbell's words, "well organized and great care had been taken in the planning although we did not know for sure what we were getting into." "The Cobb Seamount," Campbell later wrote, "was an unforgiving teacher."

CHAPTER 4

base camp

Shortly after 2 o'clock in the afternoon of October 6th, 1968, John Phillips, Captain of the research ship "Oceanographer," announced to the ship's company that they had arrived on station above the Cobb Seamount. The sea didn't look much different than the miles of ocean already traversed during the two day trip from Seattle. The sky was overcast and it was cool. The giant ship bobbed atop the swells that washed over the summit of the Seamount while off the starboard side a small buoy placed there by a Canadian team during an earlier trip to the Cobb, provided the only clue that the ship was where it should be. Since there was only one anchor deployed from the ship, Captain Phillips had to keep the vessel on station using its power and bow thrusters to maintain its position.

The "Oceanographer" was a combination luxury liner and research vessel. Her accommodations were sumptuous, with air conditioned staterooms and a large spotless galley. Yet among the creature comforts was crammed the most advanced scientific, navigation and exploratory equipment available. Commissioned just two years before, the "Oceanographer" was the largest of the Environmental Sciences Service Administration (ESSA) ships. Its function was primarily to serve as home and laboratory of the ESSA scientists as they surveyed and measured the world's oceans. On this trip the three hundred foot long floating lab was the home to the divers, scientists and technicians of Project Sea-Use.

The task of this first of four phases of Project Sea-Use was to conduct a thorough survey of the seamount including the gathering of rock and marine life samples and to determined from the survey how best to proceed with the remaining phases. As envisioned the remaining phases would include more ambitious experiments such as placing instruments and a manned habitat on the pinnacle.

Unlike the crude but effective efforts of Captan Johnson and Don Powell a decade before, bottom samples would not be taken by "tallow line," but by hand...by divers who would descend to the mountain top, gather the samples and return to the surface. Likewise the surveys themselves would be made by divers and not just the instruments aboard the ship floating above them. The preparation was not unlike that of climbing a mountain. The climbers, in this case the divers, had to be trained and conditioned while tons of supplies and equipment had to be staged and made ready for the descent.

In addition to Campbell, Eurick, Patton and White, other divers selected for phase one operations were assigned by the agencies taking part. From Honeywell Marine Systems, Chuck

Blackstock and Jim Gavin brought the engineering skills necessary to placing and maintaining instrument packages on the Cobb Summit. Another of the engineer-divers was Bob Lium of the Bellevue engineering consulting firm of Severdrupp & Parcel. Lium was a specialist in structural and civil engineering. One of the few divers not trained by Campbell was Doctor Peter Taylor, a Oceanographer from the University of Washington.

Non-diving members of the team included Doctor Merrill Spencer, Campbell's boss at the Virginia Mason Research Center who served as the team's physician. The expedition's chief scientist was Doctor Robert Burns of the Environmental Science Services Administration and the Seattle Post Intelligencer's Doug Wilson was the official photographer.

The Project Sea-Use team of divers and scientist were assigned staterooms in the forward part of the ship, one deck above the main deck. Their primary work area was aft, near the large crane that was used to hoist small boats and divers over the side. Inside the small weather shack that served as the expedition's dive station, was a small single lock decompression chamber about nine feet long and three feet in diameter. The chamber, borrowed from a consecution company in Portland, Oregon, looked a lot like a large hot water tank laid on its side. At one end was a door that resembled a pressure cooker lid that was secured by a series of "dog" cleats. Two small port holes about four inches in diameter and a single light bulb suspended from the chamber's ceiling provided the only light to the inside where a red vinyl pad stretched the chambers entire length. With barely enough room for two people, the chamber was anything but comfortable, but in the case of an emergency decompression, comfort was not high on the list of priorities…saving lives was.

Next to the diving station was a compressor used to fill the diver's tanks with air. At 130 feet below the surface divers using compressed air would have no more than thirty minutes productive work time on the bottom before they would have to return to the surface. The accumulation of nitrogen in the blood would require them make decompression stops on the way to the surface in order to prevent the "bends." For that reason compressed air dives were often limited to what were called "bounce" dives whereby divers would dive to the bottom grab whatever they were after and immediately return to the surface to avoid what they called the "D" or "decompression zone. This was deemed by Team Leader Campbell to be an unproductive use of manpower and drastically curtailed the amount of productive work. Instead Campbell ordered that subsequent dives would be "mixed gas" dives using a combination of oxygen and nitrogen which would allow divers longer bottom times and shorter decompression times on the way up. The result was working dives of thirty to forty minutes with decompression stops on the way up.

Campbell told an assembly of the divers and ship's company that evening the phase one operations would include two basic types of diving operations; SCUBA and line tended dives using surface supplied air. The latter type dive was sometimes called "hookah" because it resembled, rather remotely, the mid-eastern water pipe of the same name in that it was a single source with hoses off which several divers could breath at the same time. During those diving operations where the air was supplied from the surface, the divers received air through two second stage SCUBA mouthpieces (Regulators). As a safety measure each diver would also carry two standard seventy cubic feet compressed air tanks with regulator and mouthpiece. This would provide the divers with an emergency air supply in the event of a failure in the surface supply system. Both types of diving operations had their advantages and disadvantages. SCUBA allowed the divers more freedom to move around and was best suited for the survey work which required the divers to cover wide areas of the Seamount's pinnacle. The "hookah" apparatus while normally allowing divers to work without cumbersome tanks on their backs were limited by the length of hose from the ship above them.

The first divers in the water that first day were Chuck Blackstock and Jim Gavin. They would not actually be diving but were to man one of the Zodiacs as safety divers for the next team. The next team meanwhile began "dressing in" for their dive. Team

Leader Campbell and diver Carl Eurick were scheduled to make a reconnaissance dive to inspect an instrument package placed on the summit by the Canadian Government a year before.

First on was the wet suit made of neoprene and anywhere from a quarter to a half inch thick. It's semi-impervious construction allowed water in that was heated by the diver's own body heat. Under the wet suit the divers often wore an undergarment to help them   hold in the heat, but thanks to the Japanese Currents that washed the North Pacific Coast the water at the Seamount was an almost balmy 68 degrees. As a result the divers were able to wear the thinner suits with no undergarments. Next came the boots and hood that left only the face and the hands exposed to the cool sea air that swept across the deck of the ship.

Although this was to be a line tended dive with air hose, each diver wore SCUBA gear consisting of two tanks and a regulator mouthpiece. The added sixty pounds did little for the diver's comfort, but it was mandatory to have a back up system since, as Campbell stated, open ocean diving was risky at best and being safe was important during the dives. The last items of dive wear were the lead weights, up to twenty pounds in some cases, necessary to offset the buoyancy of the wetsuits and air tanks. The weights were strung on a fabric   belt, strapped over all the other belts and hoses so that in the case of trouble, the weights could be dropped first and fast.

Since this was a line tended dive the usual "mask" that covered the eyes and nose of the diver was replaced with a larger full face mask inside of which was a breathing mouthpiece not un- like those used when using the smaller mask. The advantage of the this type of mask over the regular mask was that the diver could, if needed release the mouthpiece in order to talk to another diver. The hose supplying air to the mask was inter-woven with the safe- ty line to prevent anyone on the surface or for that matter the diver himself from pulling the air hose free. It also lessened the chance of getting the hose tangled. The safety line and hose were attached to a harness worn by the diver with the air hose passing under the right arm of the diver to his mask. The hose from the emergency SCUBA tanks carried by the diver dangled freely under the diver's left arm, within easy reach.

Dressed in their black wetsuits, with dive fins in one hand and the air hoses and safety lines in the other, Campbell and Eurick looked more like creatures from a science fiction movie than scien- tists. The pair was already receiving air from the dive station which was being monitored by Roland White. It was his job to make sure the divers received adequate air during the dive. Once the divers were in the water and on their way to the bottom, White would have to increase the pressure from the cylinders so that the divers would get an adequate supply of air. White had calculated prior to the dive the manifold air pressure would be 120 pounds...

until the divers reached fifty feet. By the time the divers reached the bottom, the manifold   air pressure would be increased to 160 pounds This would be enough pressure   to overcome the loss of pressure on the hose line due to the pressure of the water while at the same time provide adequate pressure for the regulators

Several yards away from the ship, bobbing   in the swells, divers Blackstock and Gavin manned the Zodiac, ready to provide assistance to Campbell and Eurick should they need it. It was another of Campbell's precautions for open ocean diving…that anytime divers were in the water, there would be divers on the surface directly above them ready to help if needed.

It was decided that the pair would enter the water from the two man diving stage which was lowered into the water by the ship's crane.

As the divers entered the water, John Patton tended the air hoses and safety lines, feeding them out with just enough tension as to prevent them becoming fouled. As briefed prior to the dive, Campbell and Eurick would swim to the starboard side of the ship then move outward toward the nearest buoy that floated on the surface. Once they reached the buoy it was simply a matter of following the buoy's anchor line to the summit of the seamount. That was the plan.

But just as the two divers entered the water the ship rose on a swell, tightening the line. The coiled hoses were ripped from Patton's hands. Trouble! Patton grabbed the line and held it fast. As he did, Campbell and Eurick, instead of stopping, were suddenly swept beneath the stern of the ship. They were helpless as the ship continued to rise and fall with each swell. The strong current prevented the ship from holding station adding to the danger. The divers didn't have enough line, or for that matter enough strength to break away from the pressure of the water as it washed in and out, hammering them against the ship's hull. Patton played out the line, but it didn't help. Patton yelled "divers under the ship!" Immediately Blackstock and Gavin leaped into the water from the Zodiac and swam toward the ship. They held short however for fear of being swept under the hull like Campbell and Eurick. Aboard the ship, White grabbed a phone and notified Captain Phillips. Even though the ship was being held on station by its thrusters, the propellers were still turning due to the current and could cause injury if a diver were swept into them.

Both Campbell and Eurick continued to get air from the dive station on deck, but fear and exhaustion brought on by trying to get away from the ship's hull had driven their consumption of air to an extremely high and dangerous level. Campbell, still being held against the hull managed to drop his weight belt and with a great deal of difficulty, and was able to push himself away from the ship. He broke the surface a few feet away from Blackstock and Gavin, who grabbed him and helped him to the Zodiac. Seconds later Eurick, exhausted and gasping for air, broke the surface. Eurick had been slammed against the ship's hull several times as he made his way to the surface. He wasn't injured but the plastic helmet that held his faceplate was cracked.

Later that day, after being pronounced in good condition by Doctor Spencer, Campbell and Eurick talked to their fellow divers.

"It was like being keelhauled." Campbell told the assembled divers and scientists.

"Yeah'" Eurick added, "what really scared us was the possibility of being pulled into the propellers!"

It was clearly evident that the combination of having to keep the Oceanographer on station by using thrusters, plus the current and swells, made line tended dives from the ship very dangerous.

"From now on," Campbell stated, "we'll dive from the Zodiacs, well away from the ship."

The next morning the weather had improved only slightly. There was a low overcast, no winds and the seas were calm...except for the swells that constantly rolled over the seamount. Captain Phillips, using the ship's propellers, and bow thrusters had managed to keep the Oceanographer precisely on station throughout the night. The dive team had hoped to be well into the project by now, but the incident the day before had slowed operations. It was decided that the second of the five planned dives would be scrapped and the third would pick up where the first left off, surveying the Seamount.

After breakfast Team Leader Campbell and Roland White prepared for the dive. They would use SCUBA with compressed air, which meant both divers would, when finished, have to make two decompression stops on the way to the surface. Unlike the previous days dive, Campbell and White would enter the water from one of the Zodiacs positioned several hundred yards from the Oceanographer and make their way to the pinnacle hand over hand down the anchor line of the Canadian Buoy.

With Blackstock and Gavin again riding shotgun in another Zodiac, Campbell and White began the dive in a flurry of blue water and bubbles. They moved slowly, equalizing the pressure in their ears by blowing against their face masks. As they passed through thirty feet they could easily make out features of the pinnacle just over a hundred feet away. Gray-green plant life swayed back and forth in the strong currents that passed over the Seamount. Beneath the sea grass and other plants, black and white streaks of basalt and thousands of fish filled their field of view. Campbell mentioned later that it was like a dream world. As the two divers drew close to the bottom they could see that the top of the gigantic mountain was flat, a plateau of twenty or more acres. Two vertical walls, which would be called "cliffs" if the mountain were on land, disappeared into the blackness of the ocean.

When they reached the bottom, Campbell and White stopped and let their fins fall slowly to the surface. They stood for a moment to get their bearings, checked their watches, then after attaching a line to the Canadian Buoy anchor so they could find their way back, gave each other a thumbs up and off they went... exploring. The divers restricted themselves to a depth no deeper than 150 feet. Which meant that they could only go so far to be able to return to the ascending line before that pre-determined time on the bottom ran out. As Campbell made his way through the azure-blue water, huge fish swirling around him like giant gnats, he suddenly saw a large metal cylinder. It was about thirty feet long, four feet in diameter. It was rough and jagged on both ends indicating that it had once been part of something longer. At one end the object was uneven by several feet as if ripped apart from some terrific force. Campbell moved along the cylinder's length looking for some indication of its origin, but he had a good idea. It was, he surmised, the remains of Oregon State University's Totem ll.

Both divers knew about the Totem project and its premature end, but neither had expected to find a trace of it on the pinnacle. More likely, they thought, it should have been swept away by the strong currents that swept over the seamount. After another long pass along the Totem, Campbell signaled to White that it was time to return to the surface. The two divers slowly made their way back to the ascending line and up the anchor line just as they had come down, hand over hand. When they reached twenty feet from the surface, Campbell signaled a stop, the first of two decompression stops. The Sea-Use diving protocol, agreed to long before the ship arrived on station, specified that no dives would be made that required decompression stops deeper than twenty feet and stops no longer than ten minutes. Just before reaching the pre-designated decompression stop the divers checked watches at the twenty foot level, to make sure their bottom time was accurate. If the times were different, the decompression stop at twenty feet for ten minutes would be adjusted.

The seas around the divers were lighter as daylight penetrated the water from above. The stop seemed like hours, but was really just long enough to allow the nitrogen that had accumulated in their bodies to dissipate the same way it had accumulated, through the respiratory system. When the time was up, Campbell pointed to his watch and the pair head for the surface. At ten feet they made the second of their two decompression stops. It was much lighter and they could see the Zodiac and two divers waiting for them. It was comforting to know that even though they had not yet broken the surface, should anything happen now, their buddies were close enough to help.

When the proper amount of time had passed, Campbell and White surfaced.

CHAPTER 5

riding anchor

The following day, October 8th, the dive team having completed only two of the five planned dives, decided make yet another survey dive as Campbell and White had spent most of their time inspecting what was left of Totem ll. In order to save time, Team Leader Campbell suggested the use of a trapeze bar, a device that would allow two divers to be towed across the pinnacle, an activity he called "riding anchor."

"It's simple," Campbell explained, "sort of like fishing… we put a weighted line down to 100 feet, attach another line to a bar at about eighty feet. Then we'll use the ship's launch to pull the device over the summit while the two divers hold on t the bar!"

"It sounds simple enough," It was Carl Eurick who spoke, "but how do you know where to pull us?" Eurick and Peter Taylor had been chosen to make the dive.

"We'll use a transit search," Campbell explained. "Using the ship as a hub, we'll dispatch the launch by radio to spoked radials, each about 5 degrees apart. The resulting pattern," he said, "would resemble a giant fan.

Using a mixture of nitrogen and oxygen in their SCUBA tanks, Eurick and Taylor would have, at 90 feet, about thirty minutes to survey the pinnacle. After thirty minutes the pair would surface for a break, then "ride" for another thirty minutes. This technique would allow the divers to survey for as much as an hour without decompressing, thus doubling the time that would be allowed with a compressed air dive. Even though it took two dives to do it, the system worked and Campbell was elated. He purposed to recommend the "riding anchor" technique on subsequent search and survey missions.

The success of the dive raised morale among the ships company as well as the dive team and for the first time there was a feeling, if not a hope, that the project would be completed.

By two that afternoon preparations for the final dive were underway. The divers, Chuck Blackstock and Jim Gavin were tasked with collecting rock samples and taking pictures. Even though Campbell earlier ordered that there would be no more "line tended" dives, he recanted and allowed that this dive would be a line tended dive from the fantail of the Oceanographer.. Once in the water and well clear of the ship's propellers, they would use a descending line to reach the pinnacle. To make sure the lines remained clear, they would be tended by two other divers aboard the ship's small boat stationed several yards away from the ship. The procedures required that both divers wear buoyancy vests and SCUBA tanks in addition to the surface supplied air hose which would serve as their main air supply. The air tanks would be used only in the case of emergency.

Because the air was to be supplied from the high pressure cylinders aboard the ship, the air pressure would normally be increased as the divers descended. It was decided by Blackstock that 130 pounds of pressure would be used throughout the dive. This was in direct violation of the established procedures as 160 pounds of pressure was specified once the divers were on the bottom. The reason for the change was not clear. What was clear however was that 130 pounds of pressure was not, as Campbell would later explain, adequate to provide sufficient pressure to the regulators, which meant the divers would have to exert extra effort to breathe.

Conditions for the dive were good. The seas were running swells of four feet and the wind was about ten knots from the West. The combination of the ship's anchor, bow thrusters and propellers were enough to hold the ship steady. Not perfect but good enough for the conditions.

Blackstock and Gavin were lowered from the aft deck of the ship aboard the crane mounted diving stage. They remained on the platform until they reached thirty feet. They carefully check each others equipment…tanks, harness, weight belt, life vest…to make sure nothing was amiss. Once the check was completed the divers signaled a thumbs up to one another, pushed off the platform and swam toward the descending line which was rigged off the side of the ship. The line was weighted with a lead weight and the divers would descend the same way they had descended the buoy anchor lines, head first, hand over hand.

As the air line was played out when the divers left the platform, the ship's Executive Officer ordered the ship's propellers stopped to avoid any chance of the divers being sucked under the ship. But as soon as the "Exec" gave the order and the propellers stopped, the wind and currents began to move the ship, dragging the anchor and the divers. Realizing what was happening the Exec quickly ordered the propellers started but at a very low RPM, just enough to hold the ship in place. The ship steadied and the divers were alright. Upon reaching the end of the descending line Blackstock and Gavin stopped for a moment to adjust to their surroundings before swimming off to collect rock samples. Blackstock noted some difficulty in breathing but passed it off as exertion and excitement due, he surmised, to the environment in which he found himself. The reality was that the 130 pounds of air pressure was insufficient to provide a working respiratory rate. As the two of them moved away from the line both noticed their breathing was increasingly labored. They were simply not getting enough air. They stopped moving hoping it was nothing more than an increase in their respiratory rate because of the excitement. They breathed slightly easier now and began moving away from the line...but again their breathing became more difficult. Suddenly their infatuation with the pinnacle and the panorama before them vanished. No longer did it seem important that they were doing something that few others have done or ever will do. Their thoughts turned to the surface more than a hundred feet above them and of course... staying alive. Blackstock signaled to Gavin with an upward gesture of his arm that they had better return to the surface. Something was wrong, they knew that, but what was wrong they didn't know.

The divers turned expecting to find the descending line no farther than an arms length away, It wasn't there. It was at least fifty feet away and barely visible through the blue-green water and schools of fish. As they reached it, in what seemed like minutes but was really only seconds, their breathing difficulties worsened. Now fearing for their lives, Blackstock grabbed the line and jerked, hard! He was sure he had jerked the line five times knowing that anything over four pulls would have told the people on the ship there was an emergency and the divers wanted up... fast! But top-side, Bob Lium had felt only four jerks of the line and responded with a normal return pull and began to bring the divers up. He had no idea of the problems below.

Blackstock and Gavin were getting little if any air by now and they both knew that they would never make it at the rate they were headed for the surface. Whether it was panic or a lack of air, probably both, neither diver could find the mouthpiece for the SCUBA tanks they wore on their backs. Realizing he couldn't find it, Blackstock initiated a "bail-out" procedure. Reaching down he unbuckled his weight belt and let it fall away. Next he released the harness that held the surface supplied air hose. As he began to ascend faster he glanced back at Gavin who was still having difficulty, He was about twenty feet above him and there was nothing he could do. As he pulled the CO2 lanyards on his life vest he exhaled, the air streaming from his lungs. With the vest inflated he began to more faster toward the surface...the compressed air in lungs continued to expel. The surface seemed miles away and instead of getting lighter, it was getting darker and he began to lose conscienceless. His legs ached from the frantic kicking of his fins.

Below him, still near the bottom, Jim Gavin continued to struggle with his equipment. His a air hose harness had come free, but as it did, it became tangled with the emergency SCUBA back pack. Gavin could not locate the mouthpiece for SCUBA tanks and in his struggle found it harder and harder to breathe. Barely conscious he grabbed the descending line and began to pull himself upward, hand over hand, toward the surface. Trailing behind him was a mass of tangled hose and he realized that as he was pulling himself upward he was also bringing with him the descending line and the one-hundred pound weight that held it down. He paused long enough to reach for his knife hoping to cut himself free. He couldn't and he still had almost ninety feet to go.

By now Blackstock had broken the surface. He didn't remember the last fifteen feet of his ascent, but didn't care either as precious air filed his lungs. As he surfaced, safety diver Roland White was next to him in the water.

"Get Gavin!" Blackstock blurted, "he's in trouble."

White turned and yelled for Bob Lium to pull fast and hard. Two more divers were in the water now assisting Blackstock. Campbell, watching from the deck of the Oceanographer, ordered the crane operator to put the diving platform back into the water.

When Gavin appeared at the surface he was barely conscious and choking from the water that had entered his lungs. One of the divers held his head out of the water while the other, knife in hand, began cutting away the mass of hose and line that trailed behind him. White grabbed Gavin's regulator mouthpiece from where it had wedged between is wetsuit and life vest,, and thrust it into Blackstock's mouth. He pressed the purge button on the regulator forcing air into Gavin's lungs. Blackstock had by now regained enough strength to help his diving partner onto the lowered diving platform and the crane lifted them aboard.

Before the diving platform hit the deck, Team Physician Dr. Merrill Spencer was there and ordered the assisting divers to remove Gavin's hood and wetsuit jacket. Gavin was pale and his breathing shallow and he did not move. Dr. Spencer checked Gavin for any obstructions in his throat and kept talking to him, asking him his name, trying   desperately to get a response. There was none.

"He's non-responsive." Doctor Spencer declared. "and without his conscious confirmation, I can't tell if he has the bends or a possible air embolism." Until he could talk to Gavin, Dr. Spencer had to assume the diver was unable to expel all the air in his lungs on the way to the surface and there could be damage from trapped gases that expanded during the divers ascent. Despite his shallow breathing, Gavin's pulse was strong and his blood pressure normal. As the Doctor worked, Gavin began to regain consciousness. His eyes were half open. He tried to speak.

"Don't move," the Doctor said, "you're alright!"

"I can't move!" Gavin replied.

"Good, don't try." Spencer said.

As Gavin regained control of his senses he complained of numbness over his entire body. The Doctor judged it to be a possible embolism . Not willing to take a chance he ordered that Gavin be placed in the decompression chamber. It was standard practice really. Any symptoms following a dive, no matter the severity, called for time in the decompression chamber to make sure that any nitrogen bubbles are dissipated through the respiratory system. "I don't think there's an embolism, but lets make sure, " Spencer told Campbell. Both suspected embolism based on Gavin having no pain, but appeared to be disorientated. As the two men talked

Campbell glanced over to see Gavin suddenly go into convulsions…his head moving side to side. Campbell instinctively reached for an oxygen mask and placed it over Gavin's nose and mouth. Gavin began to calm down.

The decompression chamber was barely big enough for one man, but Campbell, now dressed down to his swimming trunks, squeezed into the chamber along side Gavin to help him through the decompression. As the dog cleats on the door of the chamber were tightened down, Carl Eurick began pressurizing the chamber. Inside the temperature began to rise and the high pitch shrill of the air flow into the chamber caused momentary discomfort to both divers. Slowly they were pressurized to a depth of about 150 feet. After about ten minutes Gavin told Campbell that the numbness had left his arms and legs and he was feeling much better. Just to make sure, the two divers followed the de-compression protocol to the letter and in a just over eighteen hours they emerged from the chamber. Gavin said he felt fine and he was hungry. Only after a thorough examination, Gavin was pronounced ok and except for a slight fever and some chills he slept through the night.

While Gavin slept, Team Leader Campbell and Blackstock had a "heart to heart" chat about the incident and just who was in charge. As team leader, Campbell made it very clear to Blackstock and later to the entire team, that he had specified a diving pressure of 160 pounds and explained that the reduced air pressure was only a problem at 130 feet and when he felt his breathing restricted he should have gone to the tanks on his back. The reduced air pressure would not be a problem as the diver ascended he explained and noted that had he not panicked he could have helped Gavin. Campbell concluded his lecture by insisting that no one but the diving supervisor, was to tell the dive station operators what pressures to set for a dive. Blackstock got the message and learned a valuable lesson…thankfully not fatal…but valuable.

With that the scientists and dive team members decided that they had done enough this trip. Besides Doctor Spencer was a little nervous about Gavin and wanted him closer to a hospital just in case there were complications.

They had made four of the five planned dives and were able to survey the mountain top with some degree of thoroughness. But the expeditions chief scientist, Doctor Burns expressed disappointment in not being able to recover the instrument packages that were placed on the summit nearly two years before. The instruments would have provided valuable information on wave and tide action in the open ocean. The recovery would have to wait, but Burns suspected the information stored in the instruments will have deteriorated by the time they return to the Cobb Seamount next summer After two days, with mixed emotion, they set sail for home.

CHAPTER 6

sea-use II

Because of the incident during the previous mission to Cobb Seamount, planners realized that more time needed to be allotted to diver training. The problem, the planners said, was too little time between missions and the Sea-Use requirement that technical personnel be included on the Sea-use 1 mission. The result was less room for the more experienced divers and there was insufficient time to train and qualify the less experienced members. The planners also suggested more attention be given to diver safety. Subsequent operations, they ruled, would require more strict diver qualifications including a rigorous underwater field training program.

Tougher physical and diving requirements were established as well and by August of 1969 a large group of aspiring Cobb divers had assembled at McCaw Air Force Station at the tip of Washington's Olympic Peninsula for a three day training program. In order to train under conditions most like those encountered at Cobb Seamount, actual diver training operations were conducted few hundred yards offshore from the decks of a U.S. Navy Tug Boat and the Coast Guard Cutter "Point Countess."

In addition to safety procedures, the would-be underwater explorers were schooled in the use of underwater tools, communications, survey techniques and a dozen other tasks they would be required to perform on the Seamount.

While Project Sea-Use officials and leaders desired to retain as many divers as possible from previous missions, only four were selected for the Sea-Use ll team at the end of the training. They were Spence Campbell, Roland White, Bob Lium, and Chuck Blackstock. Newly qualified divers were Jeffry Scott, a maritime technician from Honeywell Marine Systems, Vince Rainier representing the Northwest Diving Institute, John Goode an underwater explosives expert from Rocket Research Corporation, Charles Birkland a University of Washington marine biologist and Doctor Kent Smith, a diver and physician from the Virginia Mason Research Center in Seattle. Also joining the team was Oregon State University's Jim Washburn who, in 1968 had supervised the installation of the ill-fated TOTEM ll, the remains of which lay on the pinnacle of the Seamount.

Even with the new divers and tougher training requirements, Project Sea-Use officials felt that the program needed a bit more experience at the supervisor position, someone with more experience in open-ocean diving. Since the decision ultimately fell on the shoulders of Oceanographic Institute Executive and it's Planning Director both of whom were retired military officers, it was no surprise they had a military man in mind. After discussion with the Sea-Use Committee and the Project's Directors, it was decided to enlist the services of Robert Sheats, a retired U.S.Navy Chief Petty Officer who was, prior to his retirement, the lead diver for the Navy"'s SEALAB Underwater Habitat program. When asked to join the team, Sheats indicated he would gladly serve in the Supervisor position...as a volunteer. The Sea-Use Committee had little or no doubt that Chief Sheats was a good choice after all he had also run the support system for the Navy's SEALAB 1 Project, then served as team leader for SEALAB 11 where he lived and worked on the ocean floor for fifteen days.

Spence Campbell was assured that replacing him as Diving Supervisor was not a reflection on him or his ability. Campbell, the consummate professional wasn't phased and pledged to do whatever job assigned. His main concern, he told the committee was the safety of the divers. The remaining divers and technicians were not quite as gracious, some of them feeling that Sheats was an outsider who hadn't trained with them. What they didn't know was that Chief Sheats was a genuine war hero having survived three years as a prisoner of the Japanese during World War Two, including the Bataan death march. It would be up to him to make sure there would be no problems during this next phase of the Sea-Use program.

The planners envisioned four phases to Sea-Use ll, phase one a site survey not unlike the surveys already made but with the additional task of placing instruments on the pinnacle. Phase two, it was hoped, would provide a detailed biological and geological survey of the Seamount, while phase three would be devoted to an acoustical propagation study. All of these phases would require diving operations. The fourth and final objective was to place a permanent instrument mast atop the mountain...a mast similar to Oregon State University's Totem ll project. The mast would be constructed on shore and towed to Cobb Seamount, hopefully with greater success than Totem ll. In late August of 1969, the divers and scientists of Sea-Use ll boarded the Coast Guard Cutter "Ivy", a 189 foot long buoy tender home-ported in Astoria, Oregon. The "Ivy" which would serve as the Sea-Use ll phase one base of operations did not have the rather sumptuous accommodations found aboard the Oceanographer, their home away from home during the previous year's expedition to Cobb. The "Ivy" was a work boat, resembling a coastal freighter, which was used to place, service and retrieve Coast Guard data buoys along the Pacific Coast. A twenty-ton crane and a forty foot well-deck amidships provided the primary working space for the crew of 52.

Living quarters aboard the ship were cramped under normal conditions and the addition of fifteen scientists and divers would certainly test the dynamics of group living.

Although the stated objective of phase one was to set instrument packages on the pinnacle, Mission Director Walter Sands had a different agenda. After five trips to the Seamount Sands knew only too well the dangers of open ocean diving and the difficulties of providing the divers a secure platform from which to operate.

"We must find a way to anchor the ship," Sands told his team, "from a least two points instead of dropping the ship's anchor then steaming all the time to keep the ship from swinging."

While Sands found little disagreement among the Sea-Use Team, others felt there was little or no time to do something about it during phase one. Sands appealed to his boss, Admiral Stanley, who with more influence than money, secured from the Naval Civil Engineering Laboratory in California, an experimental explosive anchor. The anchor when attached to the pinnacle would allow a ship, no matter how large, to be securely moored above the Seamount. Along with the explosive anchor came Navy technicians who, along with the divers, were squeezed into the ship's small living space.

Under the capable command of Ivy's Captain, Ransom Boyce, the voyage outbound was routine. The scientists busied themselves preparing the instrument packages to be placed on the pinnacle, while the divers checked and re-checked their gear and attended briefings on the planned diving operations. Chief Sheats was meticulous in his preparations. as the dive team supervisor, he was taking no chances. And for the first time the subject of sharks and shark attacks was mentioned. Sharks were seen on the Seamount during operations the summer before, but the sighting were so few that little, if any, notice or for that matter precautions were taken. Sheats reminded the divers that at least a dozen varieties of shark, including an occasional Great White, prowled the waters of the North Pacific. And while most would just be curious, he told the team the potential of an attack was real. In an effort to minimize the danger and so as not to attract sharks in the first place, Sheats, with the concurrence of Captain Boyce, ordered that no garbage was to be dumped overboard while the ship was on station and that there be no fishing from the "Ivy" while diving operations were underway. As an additional safety measure, the Chief instructed all diving personnel in the use of the "shark billy," a tubular steel club about a yard long with a spike at one end. Sheats explained that under most conditions the spike would be enough to prod a curious shark away. Most of the divers, including Sheats, hoped they wouldn't have to use their "billy". In fact they wouldn't even be carried unless there was a noticeable increase in shark activity on the pinnacle.

Once on station, Captain Boyce made several passes over the Seamount in order to locate the exact center of the mountain top's upper terrace. Once that was done, a six ton concrete anchor with a buoy about the size of a garbage can attached to it was dropped over the side of the ship. Then as the scientists and divers watched, the Ivy's crew placed six smaller anchors and buoys on the outer edges of the upper terrace. They were placed at precise compass bearings from the center anchor and buoy, resembling spokes on a giant wheel. This would give the divers and scientists the ability to orient themselves both above and below the surface. Four of the divers, Jeffry Scott, Jim Washburn, Charles Birkland and John Goode entered the water and swam to each of the outer buoys. Their task was to take up slack in the anchor lines so that each buoy was directly above its anchor. It was the first official dive of Sea-Use ll

Meanwhile Chief Sheats and Bob Lium descended to the pinnacle at the center buoy. At a depth of 120 feet the visibility was about fifty feet, considerable less that what they expected. But it was good enough to do the job at hand which was to select sites from which diver-scientists could get rock samples and two sites for the explosive anchor.

The next day, as more survey dives were conducted, primarily to search for a better location for the explosive anchor, the dive team noticed a significant increase in shark activity. Eight Blue Sharks were counted, the largest about eight feet long, but they presented no danger and did not interfere with the diving operations. When several 8 to twelve foot White Tip Sharks were spotted Sheats ordered that divers will carry "shark billys" on any subsequent dives.

Two days after arriving on station, the scientists and divers could not find a better site for the explosive anchor so it was decided to make the first "shot" on a relatively flat area just a few hundred yards Northwest of the center buoy anchor. The next morning preparations for placing the anchor and its launcher on the pinnacle began. The sea state was 3, meaning waves were anywhere from one to four feet which at the higher end was only marginally for safe open-ocean diving operations. Sheats told Boyce and Walter Sands that he felt it was not safe to make the attempt under the present conditions. But Sands reminded the Diving Supervisor that time was working against them. Sheats was persuaded and ordered the operations to proceed.

While the divers were getting ready, the technicians from the Navy's Civil Engineering Laboratory and diver John Goode, the explosives expert, began preparing the explosive anchor. The anchor looked like a giant arrowhead with barbed flukes that when fired from a nine foot high launcher would actually be driven into the surface of the Seamount. That was the theory. But no one had ever fired one of these things into solid rock before. Two of the Navy technicians rode the anchor and launcher as it was hoisted over the side of the Ivy. Once over the water, the technicians would arm the launcher. Nearby, the "firing team", the divers who would actually "pull the trigger" watched from a Zodiac boat. As the anchor neared the water the two technicians were replaced by two of the Sea-Use divers who rode the anchor and launcher all the way to the surface of the Seamount. Once on the bottom, the divers released the cable and installed the detonating primer into the explosive anchor propellant then returned to the surface where they reported the launcher was sitting on a slope of about twenty-five degrees, but flat.

"That's good enough," Sands said, "let's fire it!"

In the Zodiac, firing team divers Bob Lium and John Goode had with them a device called a "hell box", a radio controlled detonator that would fire the anchor. Once their small boat was a safe distance away, Sands, standing on the deck of the Ivy, gave the signal to fire.

Goode pressed the button.

Within seconds there were lots of bubbles and a dull thud, Goode and Lium weren't sure if they heard it or felt it. Then came a rush of bubbles and a large up-welling of water above where the anchor was set.

After waiting nearly twenty minutes for the dust and debris of the explosion to settle, Chief Sheats and Jim Washburn descended to the pinnacle to see if the operation had been successful. As they made their way down the center buoy anchor line they noticed there was still plenty of debris in the water, stirred more by currents than by the explosion they guessed. As they neared the anchor they saw at once that the launcher was on its side about four yards from the anchor itself. Two of the anchor's massive barbed flukes were damaged and several barbs were missing and the rest badly bent. The two flukes had not penetrated the rock but the remaining one had penetrated the rock, not deeply, but enough so, Sheats thought, to hold the ship that steamed above them. A closer inspection however revealed a hairline crack that ran the length of the fluke and disappeared into the portion imbedded in the rock. Sheats wasn't so sure now.

Before returning to the surface to make their report, Sheats and Washburn secured a cable to the damaged launcher.

The sea state remained at two so it was decided topside to wait until morning to attempt a mooring to the anchor. But that night there was great relief among members of the diving team as they had accomplished the most difficult of their planned tasks...or so they thought. As it turned out the explosive anchor was a total failure and it was very doubtful that a ship of any size could be moored to the pinnacle using the small portion of the anchor fluke that had penetrated the Seamount. Ideally two more anchors were needed to provide the necessary three point moorage desired for Sea-Use operations. Someday, but for now the only way left to them for anchoring a ship on the surface was to use the two 9 ton concrete blocks placed on the pinnacle during earlier operations, or by using the smaller anchors of the ill-fated Totem ll

That was only one of the problems facing the Project Sea-Use team. The weather was worsening and by morning the sea state had risen to three, dashing for the time being any hopes of mooring the ship to the pinnacle. Several divers were sent to the bottom but experienced great difficulty in operating from the small Zodiac boats on the surface. After only one dive, operations were stopped to await better weather. That afternoon what remained of the explosive anchor broke loose and the Ivy began to drift away from the pinnacle. Captain Boyce ordered the engines started in order to stay as close to the mountain top as possible The storm became more intense during the night and by dawn the ship was taking waves over the bow. So intense was the storm that no one but crew members with an assignment were allowed on deck. It was like that for two days and for two days crew members and Sea-Use personnel were basically confined to quarters. The weather worsened and a sea state of 6 with waves thirteen to twenty feet forced Captain Boyce to steam away from the area just above the pinnacle where the waves were the most violent. The continuing bad weather prevented any diving and it wasn't until Sunday, August 24th that the weather cleared sufficiently to allow divers back in the water. Even though conditions for operating the small boats were marginal with thirty foot swells, Sands declared the conditions were good enough to attempt to moor the ship to what was left of the explosive anchor despite Sheats reservations. Captain Boyce maneuvered the Ivy into position while divers guided the ship's line to the partially embedded anchor fluke. With the sea state still high it would be, Captain Boyce offered, a good test of the anchor. Everyone waited anxiously to see if it would hold. It did, so Captain Boyce set the watch and the divers and crew retired for the night.

At five o'clock the next morning, Captain Boyce was awakened by the watch. The Ivy was adrift. The helmsman had, it appeared, used a radar buoy as a reference for keeping the ship on station during the night. For reason not clear, the ship had drifted over twenty miles from its position above the Cobb. Boyce ordered the ship to begin streaming to maintain its position over the pinnacle while several members of the crew hauled in the mooring line. The anchor had failed and the line had broken, due Boyce surmised to the sea state which had battered the Ivy with ten to twelve foot waves throughout the night. It was obvious from the conditions that there would be no attempt to send divers down to try and retrieve what was left of the explosive anchor...obvious to everyone but Chief Sheats. It was his feeling, a feeling he made clear to all on board, that if the Ivy were to drop her anchor and Captain Boyce steamed the ship to maintain position, diving and retrieval of the damaged anchor could be accomplished safely. Captain

Boyce however feared he'd lose the anchor in the try and said no. Sheats appealed to Sands. The answer was still no!

The next morning with calmer seas and better weather, Sheats made another appeal, suggesting this time that the divers could use the ship's anchor chain as a descending line instead of operating from the Zodiacs. Again the plan was vetoed by Boyce and Sands.

It was now Tuesday, 26 August, and except for the dive that attached the mooring cable to the explosive anchor on Sunday, there had been no diving operations on the Seamount. Morale was low. as much a result of inactivity as lack of progress on the Sea Use ll project.

Only two days remained for the Sea-Use team to accomplish the remainder of its tasks. The placing of the instrument packages on the pinnacle had been the primary goal and it was time to get with it! Sands ordered the first of the instruments lowered onto the summit. The instrument was a NUMEC Corporation beacon mounted atop a tripod and it produced a signal to which any ship might "home in" without the aid of other navigation equipment. Once on the pinnacle the beacon was tested. It worked! …for how long no one knew, but it worked now and it was a minor victory for the team. Because the sea state was still high the beacon was lowered onto the surface of the Seamount with out divers.

They would have to wait for calmer seas before securing the instrument to the basalt surface below.

Wednesday, August 27th dawned a better day. The weather had improved and the seas calmed enough to allow diving operations to resume. Sheats, quick to take advantage of the opportunity, organized his dive teams in hopes of getting all the remaining Sea-Use tasks completed. Divers Campbell and Rainier were the first away. Armed with an underwater Ram-set gun their task was to secure both the NUMEC Beacon and a NEREUS serge meter to the pinnacle. The Ram-set operated on the same principle as the explosive anchor whereby a bolt is actually fired into the rock. The serge meter was a device that would record the force of the water as it moved across the Seamount. Both instruments could be retrieved during future operations on the Cobb, that is if Campbell and Rainier could get them to stay. Much to their pleasure, the Ram-set gun worked perfectly and the instruments were secured. While they worked another team began a search for what was left of the explosive anchor in hopes of re-attaching the ship. They found it and two more divers were dispatched to the bottom with the ship's mooring line.

The last dive of the day successfully brought back rock samples from the summit and the divers joined their exhausted but happy comrades on the deck of the Ivy. Only three more dives and Project Sea-Use ll would be history.

The first dive of the last day sent two teams, Campbell and Washburn and Birkland and Blackstock back to the pinnacle to survey the TOTEM ll anchor positions, finish biological assessments, and take photographs. All four entered the water and began their descent. At thirty feet Blackstock could not clear the pressure in his ears. He stopped his descent and tried to signal Birkland who was still headed for the bottom. When he couldn't get Birkland's attention, he turned around and headed for the surface. As he broke the surface, Blackstock yelled and was immediately assisted by safety divers in a nearby Zodiac.

"Where are the others?" one of the safety divers asked.

"I signaled them," Blackstock relied, "but I'm not sure they saw me."

Once on the bottom Campbell and Washburn saw Birkland touch down, but could not see Blackstock anywhere, either on the bottom or coming down the descending line above. Campbell immediately signaled Birkland and Washburn to return to the surface.

Back aboard the Ivy a very angry Chief Sheats was watching the entire evolution. While he was mostly angry at how the entire operation was going and his inability to communicate with the scientists and ship's crew, the fact that Campbell and Washburn hadn't surfaced with Blackstock really upset him. It was the last straw and as Birkland, Campbell and Washburn made their way back to the Ivy, Sheats determined to take out his frustrations on

Campbell and Washburn. As the two divers stood on the deck before him, their hoods back and their wetsuits still dripping water, Sheats reminded them of what every professional diver knows... you never leave your buddy. He was quick and loud to point out that Birkland and Blackstock should have kept a closer watch on each other ...and that Blackstock should have signaled Birkland and the first sign of trouble. Washburn couldn't help but wonder why Sheats was upset with he and Campbell when it was Blackstock and Birkland who should be hearing this. Campbell knew why however. Sheats was a Navy guy and believed in the chain of command. With Campbell as the Assistant Diving Supervisor, Sheats figured the message would get passed down.

His frustrations vented, Sheats turned to the job at hand and dispatched Lium, Roland White and Dr. Kent Smith to the pinnacle to get some rock samples...a "no sweat" dive. Doctor Smith was the least experienced of the three, but Sheats and Campbell felt it would be good for Smith who until now had been devoting all of his energies attending to the diver's medical needs, which for the most part were seasickness and headaches. But anybody who dives knows that "no sweat" dives are not without peril. In fact there is no such thing as a "no sweat" dive. To begin, all three of the divers were dropped off at the wrong buoy by the crew in the Zodiac and as a result went down the wrong descending line. When they reached bottom, Smith headed in the wrong direction. White and

Lium quickly went after him to try to get him back on course. After only six to ten minutes the three divers surfaced. Sheats couldn't believe it. But he had already spent his frustration and could only remind the three that foul ups like that are why we do pre-dive planning. Yet another entry for his lessons learned list. Blackstock meanwhile complained about being dizzy, most likely from the morning's incident with his regulator. An examination by Dr. Smith revealed nothing, but he ordered that Blackstock be kept under close observation for the next several hours to make sure.

The long strenuous hours put in by the divers in making up for lost time were beginning to take their toll. Morale was better, tempers were not. It appeared that personality conflicts were hampering operations; the result of a battle of wills between Captain Boyce, Chief Scientist Sands and Sheats. Only when Boyce and Sands allowed the divers to plan the diving operations, did the missions seem to go better.

On the final day of diving tempers and patience seemed to run out, maybe because everyone was tired, but more likely because everyone was anxious to get home. The remaining task was to recover the explosive anchor or what was left of it. Both Boyce and Sands thought it would be a good idea to have other divers descend at the same time to check out and make adjustments to the instruments place on the pinnacle earlier.

"It can't be done!" Sheats said rather emphatically, "we're running out of time. The frustration in Sheats voice was evident. He apparently could not make Boyce and Sands understand the repetitive dive table. Each time a diver went below the surface, he explained, the diver accumulated nitrogen in his system. Many of the divers had already reached their time limits as indicated by the repetitive dive table and they could not dive again, not without excessive decompression. There was little time for that, he added. The only way left to purge the nitrogen from their bodies was through normal respiratory activity at sea level pressure. For the remaining divers who hadn't exceeded their down-time limits, it was doubtful they could accomplish an meaningful work in the time they could spend on the bottom. However a compromise was reached and Sheats agreed to allow those divers with the most time remaining on their repetitive dive schedule to work until they reached their maximum open-water decompression time which would require them to make decompression stops on the way up from the bottom.

Sheats found it difficult to explain all that without losing his patience or temper. He couldn't. But the bottom line was that Sheats was the Diving Supervisor and the ultimate decision was his since he was responsible for the safety and well being of the Sea Use Divers. He didn't think any life should put in jeopardy for what he considered clean-up work. Whether Boyce and Sands understood that, it didn't matter. But as far as he was concerned the issue was settled. Now it was time to turn-to and recover the launcher.

Despite their fatigue, divers Campbell and Rainier descended to the pinnacle dragging behind them a cable from the Ivy. As they secured it to the launcher the deck crew above wound the other end around a capstan on the ship. Then on Sheat's signal power was applied to the capstan. Nothing! The launcher didn't budge. They tried again and again and nothing. After several attempts, Sheats ordered the lifting operation stopped.

"What do we do now?" a crew member asked.

There was no answer, Sheats was thinking. After several minutes, Sheats turned to Captain Boyce.

"What about the anchor chain?" Sheats asks.

"What about it?" Boyce asked in return. Why does everybody answer a question with a question Sheats thought to himself.

"Well", Sheats said, "we could attach the line to it and the crane and by using both of them might get the launcher to move." It wasn't a bad idea...certainly worth a try.

Once all lines were secure the lift began. After each pull the cable was attached to the deck rigging. Sheats figured several incremental pulls would do the job, but after the third pull the cable went slack. The connection at the launcher end had parted. Several attempts were made to re-connect the cable, but each time the fittings failed and the line parted.

By now the divers were exhausted and had reached their decompression limits. Sheats decided to forgo any additional attempts to raise the launch vehicle. That, he said, will be left to another team, another time. Sheats told his divers to clean up, and reported to Captain Boyce his decision. It was time to go home.

CHAPTER 7

man in the sound

Once home, divers, scientists and technicians turned to the routine life ashore; tending to jobs and to the more simple but no less important task of attention to family and friends. It would be six months before preparation for another assault on Cobb Seamount would begin.

Faced with the prospect of another Sea-Use phase without adequate funds, many of the Sea Use participants felt it was probably a good idea to do something about it...but what? One thing on which they all agreed was that a greater awareness of their efforts on the Cobb and man-in-the-sea projects in general was a key to better funding. Federal dollars were slow in coming, if at all and the other Sea-Use participants weren't awash in cash. What was needed, they stated, was something spectacular enough to draw both public and media attention away from "space" long enough to convince government leaders that investing in the exploration of the oceans would be wise. The project, or whatever idea they came up with would also have to tie directly into the Sea-Use program and have some scientific value.

After several weeks of mental gymnastics the media representatives to the Sea-Use program, apparently having more vision than technical expertise, suggested that a manned underwater habitat in Puget Sound might just be the ticket. After all the Sea Use program called for such an installation on the Seamount in the future. The idea was spectacular alright and it certainly met the criteria of relating to Project Sea-Use. But what about the costs…could it be done inexpensively? One of the technicians asked if it could be done at all.

"We can do this," Campbell answered, " we have the technical expertise right here…and as for costs, well we've been exploring the Cobb Seamount without a lot of money. I don't see why we can't do the same here in the sound," he added, "as long as it's not too sophisticated."

All agreed, a habitat it shall be!

Undersea habitats were nothing new, of course. The Navy's Sea-Lab project was probably the best known. And famed Oceanographer Jaques Cousteau's televised adventures of living under the sea had added a great deal of credibility to such endeavors. While Campbell's notion of being not too sophisticated would be an underlying theme, the habitat could not be just a "stunt". It had to work and be of some scientific value, so it too would have credibility.

During the design phase of the habitat in the Spring of 1969, the participants realized they had yet to name the project. After all a catchy name would go along way toward making the project appealing to the public and the media. The process proved to be a bit more difficult than the idea itself, with everyone including an ever growing cadre of non-participants, offering an idea. "House in Green Water," "The Diver's Den" and "Neptune's Nook," were just a few of the names put forth. They were not very scientific and according to Campbell, didn't capture the imagination very well. It was again left to the media members of the Sea-Use team to come up with a name..."Man In The Sound." It was perfect, not only short and catchy, just what the television news people liked, and was close enough in name to "Man In The Sea" projects underway in other parts of the world, which gave it credibility.

The design team believed a small habitat in relatively shallow water and easily accessible from shore would be ideal for this "do-it-yourself" scientific project. Campbell called upon Retired Admiral Emory Stanley, his friend and planning director for the Oceanographic Institute of Washington. Campbell knew just what he wanted and asked the Admiral to help the team convince the US Navy to give them a surplus net buoy, a large steel sphere that at one time was used to hold up submarine nets at the entrance to Puget Sound. The Navy said okay, but since they didn't deliver, the Man-in-the-Sound team had to pick it up. The 58 inch in diameter steel ball fit perfectly in the back of Roland White's pick-up truck and was carted off to White's garage.

The "Ball" as it was called, was badly in need of paint as it had spent most of its time in an outdoor storage area. But first some sandpaper and elbow grease was in order. At the same time a crew armed with cutting torches and a couple of boxes of welding iron, began cutting ports in the side of the ball and welding to it a three foot "neck" which would serve as the entry way into the habitat once it was submerged. Air hose fittings were attached to the top of the ball as was a large chain and connections for communications and power lines. On the neck itself the technicians welded hooks on which to hang SCUBA gear.

Inside the ball donated audio and video equipment was installed, and a couple of benches on which the inhabitants were to sit during their stay. The sphere was barely big enough to hold two SCUBA divers, without their tanks. They would have to leave their tanks "on the porch" before entering. That's what the outside brackets were for. Once inside the ball the divers would have no problem with air as it was forced into the habitat from an air hose attached to a compressor on shore. The air pressure would also keep water from entering the habitat and allow the divers a dry, if not warm and cozy place to abide. It was like putting a glass upside down in water, creating an air bubble in the glass.

Instead of two divers "living" in the habitat for a long period of time, the plan called for thirty-six divers to occupy the habitat in three hour shifts...around the clock for three days. Each of the participating divers, in addition to their time in the habitat, were required to make what were called excursion dives from the sphere to perform various tasks.

When the electrical and mechanical systems had been installed and checked, all that remained was a coat of red paint, to protect the ball and make it easy for the divers to see in the sometimes murky water of Puget Sound. Once painted the sphere was literally rolled back on to Roland White's pick-up truck for the trip to the dive site.

Finding a location for the Habitat was less challenging than building it. The site selected was just off a popular fishing wharf north of the Community of Edmonds, Washington. In the spirit of keeping costs down, use of the wharf was donated by its owner Jim Haines, himself a great supporter of ocean exploration and a member of the "Man-In-The-Sound " planning group.

The Haines Wharf had been the scene of previous oceanographic activity, namely the placement of a steel mast about 150 yards from shore on which the University of Washington had installed various measuring devices, most notably an instrument to measure wave heights. The site was perfect. The Wharf provided an ideal staging area for the habitat and its support equipment and the three underwater legs of the mast were just right for the habitat which was to be suspended from there about 40 feet below the surface The wharf was also equipped with an elevator which was used to launch fishing boats. It was perfect for launching the habitat. In a small anteroom in the wharf's storage area, the Man-In-The-Sound team set up a small life support system not unlike the system used during the Cobb Seamount expeditions. The system included air monitors, communications equipment, including a television monitor that was connected to a small underwater camera which would allow technicians and just about anyone interested to watch the divers move in and out of the habitat. Once the air and communications lines were attached to the shore based life support system, they were dragged by small boat to the mast to await the habitat. It was time.

In the afternoon of November 8, 1969, Sharon Dodge, an instructor at Northwest Diving Institute, officially started the Man-In-The-Sound project by christening the habitat with a bottle of champaign. When the applause and congratulations died down the divers entered the water and technicians using the elevator slowly lowered the sphere into the water. Towing the habitat to the mast took over an hour even though it was just a little over a football field away. A small boat inched the sphere along while six divers kept the ball upright to keep it from rolling on its side and filling up with water. The last thing anyone wanted to happen was to have the "ball" sink. Attaching the habitat to the mast was, happily, a lot easier that anticipated. All lines were attached and just enough water to ensure mutual buoyancy was allowed into the sphere. By regulating the amount of air and water the divers were able to regulate the rate of descent and place it exactly where they desired… about 40 feet deep and in the center of the three legs of the University's instrument mast. Once in position the sphere was attached to the mast with a chain.

While there were no official sponsors of the Man-The-Sound Project, other than Northwest Diving Institute, there were plenty of official fans. The Virginia Mason Research Center led a long list of enthusiastic supporters which included the Pacific Science Center, Bellevue and Shoreline Community Colleges, the Washington Council of Skin Diving Clubs, the National Association of Underwater Instructors, KOMO-TV and the Washington State Oceanographic Commission, a sponsor of Project Sea Use. It appeared that the criteria of raising awareness of man-in-the-sea programs would be easily met. It was hoped by the Man-In-The-Sound team, the project would at the same time attract personalities who could provide either support or influence those who could provide support. Among those visitors to the Haines Wharf site was U-S Congressman Lloyd Meeds who represented the district in which the event was being conducted. He was so taken by the nature of the project that he made several visits to the site. On one of those visits the Congressman presented the divers and technicians an American Flag that had flown above the US Capitol. It was immediately raised on the mast above the submerged habitat.

Another frequent visitor was Doctor Dixy Lee Ray, Director of Seattle's Pacific Science Center, herself a noted marine biologist and member of the Washington State Oceanographic Commission. She would one day become the Governor of the State of Washington, but sadly too late to positively impact the financial concerns of Project Sea-Use.

Despite the voluntary nature of the Man-In-the-Sound project. Campbell as the man in charge, ran it like he ran the initial dives on Project Sea-Use 1. There was a clear chain of command, lines of authority and accountability. "This is serious business," Campbell proclaimed, "we want everything to go smoothly." He set the pace and the tone for the entire operation and high on the list of his priorities was safety, Qualified personnel would be on duty, twenty four hours a day, for the length of the project. And Campbell explained that only after a fifteen hour check and recheck of all systems were made that the habitation would begin.

The first to occupy the habitat was the distaff team of Sharon Dodge and Diane Parypa. A qualified advanced diving instructor and mother of three, Mrs. Dodge, when asked via radio what it felt like to be inside the habitat said "it's a lot like being inside a softball. It even has seems," she added. Both women said they had enough room but, adding a bit a feminine humor, said the sphere could use a little more cupboard space. Like all inhabitants would do, Dodge and Parypa made excursions from the sphere,

Dodge to collect samples for the local community college and conduct water salinity studies, Parypa, a Mercer Island, Washington High School teacher, used the time outside to sample some of the marine life around the habitat.

During the time the two occupied the habitat, the Puget Sound region was rocked by an earthquake, a small one but strong enough to be measured by the University of Washington Seismology Lab. While the waiting dive teams and technicians on the wharf definitely felt the structure move back and forth, Dodge and Parypa said they could feel the sphere swaying, but thought it might have simply been the ocean currents

While the dive teams shuttled back and forth between the habitat and the wharf, interested citizens who often followed the project on the media, frequently dropped by to watch the television monitors on the wharf and check on the progress of the Man-In-The-Sound project, at times even chatting via radio with the divers inside the sphere. During the three days that the habitat was in the water over 100 visiting divers were given tours of the habitat and its support equipment, many of them earning extra credit for college diving and oceanographic studies.

In addition to the sampling and biological studies of the marine life around the habitat, one of the more "tricky" tasks was the recovery of a small instrument package dropped into the Sound near the habitat from an airplane. The instrument package was equipped with a sounding device that emitted a constant tone. Though it was nighttime, it took a dive team just seventeen minutes to find and recover the package. The importance of this excursion, according to Campbell, was to test the feasibility of dropping supplies to divers working on the Cobb Seamount during the next phases of Project Sea- Use.

As in life nothing lasts forever and too soon it was over. The participating divers and technicians assembled their equipment and headed for home The sphere was taken off the mast and like before rolled into the back of Roland White's pick-up truck.

Campbell, like most of the participants, was elated with the project. He boasted that during the three day habitation no problems were noted with divers or equipment.

"It was a great success," he said, then proclaimed, "the significance of the Man-In-The-Sound project was that it was the world's first cold water habitation and was perfect for training future Seamount divers by exposing them to the extremely cold waters of Puget Sound, water that rarely rose above fifty degrees.

While the project met the criteria for creating publicity for man-in-the sea projects and Project Sea-Use in particular, its impact on the financial future of Project Sea-Use, was not yet clear. However it is likely the Sea-Use Program might not have gone as far as it did without the Man-In-The-Sound exercise.

CHAPTER 8

the chain link highway

While home both scientists and divers devoted time to assess the successes and failures of the Sea-Use ll mission. It was generally agreed that the biggest problem during the August trip to Cobb, bad weather not-with-standing, was orientation…where to descend onto the Seamount and to know where the divers were when they got there. The surface buoys and the pinger placed on the pinnacle earlier were of great assistance for the ship and small boats, but for the divers determining their exact location while on the pinnacle was still just a guess at best.. Solving that problem would be a top priority for Sea-Use lll, the 1970 excursion to Cobb Seamount.

It was also during this interim that the first hint of a scientific conflict arose. Walter Sands, the Chief Scientist for Sea-Use ll suggested that a biological census be taken during Sea-Use lll to determine the extent of marine life on the mountain. Sands pointed out that there is distinct biological cycle that could be impacted by any construction on the pinnacle. Sands wanted that to be a priority as well. Resolution of the conflict, it would seem, would have to wait until the Sea-Use lll team was on station.

After Sea-Use ll, Chief Sheats, noting Campbell's diving skills and rapport with the divers and technicians, recommended that he be reinstated as the Diving Supervisor on Sea-Use lll and subsequent missions to the Seamount.

Project Sea-Use lll , the largest full-scale assault on the Cobb Seamount, was divided into three phases, each with its own specific scientific or engineering goal. The first phase, Sea Use lll-A was to locate and recover all the instruments that were placed on the pinnacle during the previous missions. Sea Use lll-B was a back-up mission of sorts that would hopefully accomplish what phase lll-A did not. And Sea-Use lll-C would be devoted to establishing a permanent ship mooring system, a task yet to be accomplished to the satisfaction of those using the Cobb Seamount.

Sea-Use lll was to begin in May of 1970, but Spring rains delayed the departure of the US Coast Guard Cutter "Cactus" and the Sea-Use Team until May 13th. Even with the delay the team was anxious to get to the Cobb and find out what the instruments left on the pinnacle would tell them. For the most part the Sea-Use team of divers and technicians was the same as the previous mission...with one notable exception. Chief Bob Sheats was not among them but had recommended that Campbell be reinstated as the Diving Supervisor. In addition, because the Sea-Use program was designated an Oceanographic Expedition, there needed to be an official chief scientist. Campbell was selected to fill that role as well.

Diving operations began immediately after the "Cactus" arrived on station. Much to the disappointment of both the ship's company and the divers, eighteen sorties to the Cobb's surface over the first several days produced little. Hampered again by bad weather and a plankton bloom that reduced visibility to almost zero, few of the anticipated tasks were accomplished. Then two days before the team was to set sail for home the weather cleared, as did the water, and the divers headed for bottom once again.

Unlike previous missions where the divers entered the water from small boats several yards from the support ship it was determined that jumping into the water from the buoy deck of the "Cactus" might work without endangering the divers. The Buoy Deck was the working space on the Buoy Tender and only a few feet from the water, It worked, thanks in no small part, to the former "Ivy" Skipper, Ransom Boyce, who now captained the "Cactus." He would slowly maneuver the "Cactus" up to the dive site, allow the divers to enter the water and begin their descent, then back the ship off to a safe distance. The method worked just fine, it was safe and saved the expedition a lot of time. About the only difficulty was walking on the ship's pitching desk with eighty pounds of equipment and fins. The technique would not, however, work for getting the divers back on the ship. Once the divers were fin-

ished with their mandatory decompression stops, they would surface and with each hanging over the side of the Zodiac, be taken
back alongside the "Cactus" then hoisted aboard via the platform
or stage. Using small boats and a crane hoisted stage for recovery
was still the safest.

The diving day began as all dive days had begun...wake up
call at 5:30am...set up the diving systems (tanks, lines, communication) then breakfast, a pre-dive briefing and the often laborious
task of "dressing in", putting on the wet suits, tanks, safety tanks,
life vest, weight belt, mask and fins...all in time to begin diving
operations by 8 am. As in most diving operations at Cobb, Two to
three divers descended to the pinnacle with two more divers above
them in a Zodiac for safety. Because of the decision made earlier,
line dives or those tended from the ship were no longer used. The
divers entered the water from the ship and used the buoy line to get
to the pinnacle. It was during these dives that Supervisor Campbell, Kirby Johnson from Northwest Diving Institute, and lead
divers Roland White John Erickson and Vince Rainier developed
what they called the "free ranging" technique. With the aid of a
line from the safety Zodiac on the surface to the divers below, their
decompression stations and "pony bottles" would always be above
the divers no matter where they traveled on the pinnacle. The safety divers in the Zodiac would simply follow small buoys called
"popper" buoys attached to and towed by the divers. This added

not only to the safety, but to the divers peace of mind knowing they didn't have to use up valuable air traveling to and from a stationary descending line. During the "free ranging" excursions the divers would mark points of interest with small inflatable buoys which they attached to whatever they found, The divers would then send the small buoys to the surface where the safety divers in the Zodiac would attach a more substantial buoy to mark the spot. During this exercise large rock fish, in the neighborhood of 30 to 35 pounds would sometimes eat the small inflatable maker buoys as they ascended. After several had been devoured by the fish it was determined that escorting the small buoys through the first twenty-five feet of their ascent, was prudent.

As it turned out Rock Fish weren't the only concern for the divers. It was at a decompression station, about twenty feet below the surface, where Campbell looking to the surface saw one of the safety divers frantically trying to get his or his dive partner's attention. It was John Erickson. He was waving his arms and pointing to the open ocean. Campbell looked. In the distance a small black dot…whatever it was, it was moving toward them. In what seemed like seconds the black dot morphed into a large fish. It was a Great White Shark. Even though he was accustomed to all sorts of dangerous marine life, Campbell froze just staring at the shark. He said later that it was like "being bait on a hook," with no protection. Kirby Johnson meanwhile was looking the other way and didn't see the animal which Campbell later described as being about sixteen to eighteen feet long with jaws that spanned at least three feet. The two divers were back to back. It was a non-bounce dive and the two divers were just taking a two minute safety stop. when Johnson wheeled around and came face to face with the Great White. He too froze. The shark swam past them, turned about and dove away. In seconds they could see the shark coming up toward them again. By that time the two had regained their composure and although they couldn't verbally communicate with each other, they both were thinking the same thing...safety stop or not..."we're outta here"!

As Campbell broke the surface and began climbing into the Zodiac, Erickson, now in the water, saw the Great White coming up at them from about 60 feet."He's coming back'! he yelled. They could see the shark's fin as it sliced though the surface of the water. It was as big as a small sailboat, or so it seemed.

"Give us the pony bottles"! Campbell yelled. The shark was now about fifty feet away coming straight for them as the Zodiac Crew handed Campbell and Johnson the bottles. Campbell didn't need to tell Johnson what to do. As the shark approached, Erickson started a free-dive down toward the on-coming shark with his "shark billy" in hand. Fearing the shark was about to take a bite out of Erickson, Campbell and Johnson opened the pony bottles sending streams of compressed air bubbles at the shark. It worked! The shark turned tail and dove back toward the bottom. Campbell, Johnson and Erickson didn't wait to say goodbye but headed to the Zodiac. They managed to get into the boat, double dive tanks, weight belts and all, without any help. The trio found out later that the crew of the "Cactus" watched the entire incident from aboard the ship which was some distance away. One crew member, they learned, was on the bridge with a high powered rifle...just in case. It's questionable that the shooter aboard the ship would have done much good, it was decided that on subsequent missions divers would carry the lethal M-16 Bang Sticks instead of the "shark billys."

The incident would have been a fitting end to the mission, but the main objective of retrieving all the instruments from the pinnacle had not been achieved. Never-the-less it was time to go home. Captain Boyce, managed to get permission to stay one more day however and the next morning after the Great White's visit, it was back to business. Most of the briefing room chit-chat was about captain "Ahab" Campbell and the Great White!

The divers were not prepared for what they found when they finally located the instruments. It looked like a war zone. None of the instruments was in the place where they were originally set and the NEREUS serge meter while still anchored to the surface was so badly damaged that no useful information could be obtained from it. What caused the damage was not clear. Some of the scientists thought the fishing nets of foreign trawlers might have snagged the instruments and dragged them over the pinnacle as many of them were found hundreds of yards from where they were placed. Others, the divers primarily, were convinced it was the powerful currents that swept the mountain top that caused the damage. That was saying something since the instruments were not only designed to operate at great depths and strong currents, but they had been securely fastened to the Seamount using explosive bolts. Other instruments, place on the pinnacle the year before and the launcher for the explosive anchor, were located. The NUMEC pinger however was never found. Sadly none of the instruments lasted long enough to provide scientists with any valuable information.

The NEREUS Surge meter, when found, provided the team with one of the expedition's lighter moments. The meter was about three feet high with a wire mesh cap protecting the actual measuring part of the instrument. Apparently not long after it was placed on the Seamount a small fish, seeking safety from predators, swam into the cap. The currents provided ample food for the fish so there was no reason for him to move. And he didn't. When the divers found the meter, they found the fish, now far too big to escape the wire mesh cap. The life lesson wasn't lost on the team. Even though the instrument, fish and all, actually recorded what it was supposed to record, the presence of the fish inside the cap skewed the information and it wasn't usable.

Despite that and the condition of the instruments they did find, Project Sea-Use lll-A was a great success. Not only were the instruments recovered, but the divers managed, in the short time they had, to place two large anchors on the pinnacle which would be used to anchor ships in the future. They also completed the most comprehensive survey of the Seamount's summit to date. As a result it was clear Project Sea Use lll-B would not be necessary. So it was time to head for home and begin work on the next voyage.

Project Sea-Use lllC

Project Sea-Use lll-C was the largest and first federally funded mission, which until now had been a totally regional effort funded by the agencies engaged in specific tasks. Back in March of 1969, the Sea Use Council and its agent the Oceanographic Institute of Washington applied to the defense Department's Advance Research Projects Agency (ARPA) for a grant of $54,000. Acceptance of the request by ARPA was due in part that for the first time the council's application contained references to the possible military use of the Cobb Seamount. Until now the regional nature of the project excluded any direct military participation, although the US Navy , Coast Guard and the Maritime Administration had been involved as interested observers or suppliers. The ARPA grant not only made reference to the advantages of a permanent mooring system on the pinnacle but declared;

> "...the mooring system provides a toe hold for on-going projects having future military applications".

Just what "military applications" ARPA had in mind wasn't clear. What was clear however was that the military was eyeing the Cobb, made evident in a speech by the Navy's Vice Admiral T. S. Caldwell

> "A potential future project that could be of significance to the United States and a gigantic opportunity for additional business is the establishment of an ocean laboratory on one of the various seamounts."

It could accurately be assumed that the reference to "one of the various seamounts" meant the Cobb since it was the only one that could easily be reached.

The plan for establishing the mooring system was to simply drill three holes into the pinnacle, put some rock bolts and shackles in the holes, then add cement. The rock cores from the drilling were to be recovered for geologic studies. The idea was simple alright, if done on dry land, but to do so in 130 feet of water was another matter. A special rock-coring drill just for the Seamount had to be designed as did a device to test the bolts and shackles one they were secured to the mountain top.

Months later, following engineering tests, divers and scientists boarded the Coast Guard Buoy Tender "Cactus" for another trip to the Cobb Seamount. For most of those participating, it was their second trip. By now the core team of divers and technicians were veterans of open ocean diving. Never-the-less, scientists and engineers seeking to carry out diving project on the Cobb Seamount were required to attend the annual qualification and training programs as well as pass written, physical and medical diving tests.

It was to be a two ship operation and the diver's initial objective was to prepare a mooring system for the second ship. This was done by repositioning the anchors that held the ill-fated Oregon State University TOTEM in 1968. The anchors when repositioned would provide a three-point anchoring system for a ship above. This was especially important for the second ship from which the drilling operations were to be conducted. A stable platform was needed.

Before the arrival of the second ship, the "Cactus" proceeded to lay eighteen hundred feet of chain across the summit from East to West. The chain, marked off in one hundred foot sections, would serve as a highway of sorts and solve the problem of orientation on the Seamount. In what could only be described a a bit of aquanaut humor, a couple of the divers created and posted a sign at one of the decompression stations which read "Cactus Avenue and Aquanaut Street." The other side read "Japan 2,416 milers and Washington State, 240 miles."

About 800 feet of the chain was draped over the Eastern edge of the pinnacle to be used by divers as a guide to the slopes below the pinnacle. Fitting with the Project Sea-Use budget limitations, the chain was surplus anchor chain from a World War ll battleship obtained from the US Navy…at no cost. In the final report on the rock coring operations, Captain Griff Evans Jr., Executive Director of the Oceanographic Institute noted the chain link highway would prove to be a major asset in future Cobb operations.

Unlike previous trips to the Cobb, this time the weather was beautiful; sunshine, calm seas, water temperature near 70 degrees and most importantly, for some of the team anyway, no sharks!

Shortly after completing the chain link highway, the second ship, a small coastal freighter the FS 313, rendezvoused with the "Cactus". The FS 313, a work ship operated by the Washington National Guard, carried the drilling apparatus and commercial divers from Ocean Systems, to do the actual drilling. Because the drilling equipment was aboard the FS 313, it was decided that diving operations would best be conducted from it while the Coast Guard's "Cactus" served as the command vessel.

On the morning of July 30th, 1970, drilling operations began by divers from Ocean Systems Incorporated, manufacturers of the drilling equipment being used. Because the drilling require very little movement, the divers wore light weight "hard Hats" with surface supplied   air enabling them to remain underwater longer than if they had used SCUBA gear. The drilling rig required several hydraulic and handling lines which would be handled by the Army ship's crew. Despite the density of the Seamount's basalt, drilling operations went faster than expected. A faulty gauge told the engineers they were making slower progress than they really were, but after several hours they discovered they had drilled the required fifty-five inches. Then using a special "grout injector" they forced cement into the hole in which a bolt and shackle had been placed. Meanwhile the scientists topside were ecstatic over the cores that had been taken from the holes and brought to the surface. They would be analyzed.

During the next two days the second and third cores were drilled and the anchor bolts cemented in place. The drilling rig had to be brought back aboard the FS 313 after each hole was drilled so that the cores could be removed and the bit replaced. The calm seas made this task much easier.

During the drilling two of the cranes aboard the FS 313 were used, one to hold the rock coring drill and the other to raise and lower equipment from the ship's hold. For the most part the operation went smoothly, that is until a crane operator from the ship's crew managed to get on the wrong controls. He was about to lift the coring drill while it was operating. Diving Supervisor Campbell saw what was happening and was able to stop the crane operator just in time.

By morning of the third day, the first bolt had set for nearly seventy-two hours and was ready for testing. Placed over the set anchor bolt, the testing device would exert a vertical pull of one hundred and ten tons. Divers Campbell and Vince Rainier descended to the pinnacle, guided the tester to the bolt and hooked it to the bolt. A small gauge on the testing device would read out the pounds of pull as the divers took turns working the hydraulic pump handle.

After two days and twenty-eight separate dives, the testing was completed and despite the fact that at a reading of 50 tons pull one bolt withdrew about an inch and a half, the tests were pronounced a success by the engineers. However engineers were not sure the system would hold large ships, like the Oceanographer the ship used in Sea-Use 1, so additional testing was abandoned. However a much needed two point mooring system on the Cobb Seamount was in place at long last.

Almost three years had passed since Project Sea-Use planning began. The timetable had called for the establishment of an instrument mast on the pinnacle, followed by a manned habitat. When those plans were written however, few knew what to expect two hundred and forty miles off the coast of Washington State, so it was not surprising that each mission to the Cobb, new and un-foreseen problems were encountered, problems that called for new and innovative solutions. The process of gaining knowledge, ap-plying it and moving on was as slow on the Cobb as it was in any laboratory.

With the anchor bolt in place, the Sea-Use council declared the most difficult tasks of all had been accomplished and they could now proceed with the original Sea-Use timetable.

As the summer of 1970 drew to a close, the Oceanographic Institute applied to the National Science Foundation to establish a National Seamount Station in hopes of generating international in-terest and money for Cobb Seamount and Project Sea-Use. The application asked for a grant of seventeen million dollars. Contin-gent upon the NSF grant was a pledge from Washington Governor Dan Evans of an additional one-hundred thousand dollars in State funding. The timing was right, Institute members thought, since many countries of the world were participating in a ten year study of the world's oceans called the International Decade of Ocean Ex-ploration. However instead of benefitting the project, the applica-tion resulted in several of the Sea-Use participants dropping out of the project. Honeywell Marine Systems and Battelle Laboratories were private companies with contracts with the military and other Federal agencies. Should Cobb be designated a National Seamount Station, the firms believed there would be a conflict of interest should they continue their association with the Cobb Seamount program. As a result the firms withdrew from participating in Project Sea-Use, leaving the Sea-Use Council holding an almost empty bag. As it turned out the National Science Foundation did not fund the National Seamount Station, but the civilian firms elected to stay out of it anyway, probably because the country was entering a recession and many businesses were pulling back hoping to avoid the monetary crunch that was to come in the months ahead. Project Sea-Use was, it would seem, a luxury they could no longer afford.

In November of 1970, the Sea-Use Council convened a scientific summit to which it invited all the Sea-Use Participants. The purpose of the meeting was to determine just what direction the Sea-Use Council should take with respect to Cobb Seamount and find out from the scientific community what was and wasn't important about it. Everyone agreed the Seamount was a valuable scientific asset, but that a re-prioritization was in order. Instead of placing a manned habitat on the mountain top, as envisioned early on, more functional activities should be undertaken. Foremost among those more functional activities was environmental monitoring and forecasting. The participants, using data supplied by ARPA, also determined that the pinnacle plateau could not support a permeant undersea station because of heavy seas that often swept the Seamount.

Coincidental to the change of direction for Project Sea-Use and withdrawal of sponsors, was the growing concern for liability. The Executive Director of the Institute, Griff Evans had, in the past voiced his opinion that the liability waivers signed by the Sea-Use Divers weren't worth the paper on which they were written. He further contended that the Institute's Board of Trustees was ultimately responsible for any deaths or injuries on Cobb Seamount. Evans felt that was more responsibility than he or the board wanted to take, so he named a committee to study the issue. The committee reached the same conclusion as Evans and the Oceanographic Institute, which after serving nearly four years as the agent for the Sea-Use Council, withdrew its services and was replaced by the Sea-Use Foundation. The establishment of the Foundation merely took the State of Washington and its member representatives "off the liability hook"!

The Sea-Use Council meanwhile continued to function as the governing body of the Sea-Use program.

Whatever the scientific priority, there was a certain amount of urgency for returning to the Cobb Seamount. The divers and engineers had successfully laid the chain link highway and in doing so, solved once and for all the problem of orientation. But even with holes drilled and the anchor bolts grouted to the pinnacle, the open ocean mooring system remain essentially untested. The next trip would hopefully be the first ever diver assisted open ocean mooring of a ship.

CHAPTER 9

scallops

Two missions to the Cobb Seamount were authorized for 1971, without NSF funding. Somehow, planners thought they could make it work on a shoestring budget, after all they've been doing that since the program began in 1969. Like any "mountain climb" preparations were meticulous including the prepositioning of equipment and diver training.

Divers for Sea-Use IV were selected from members of the Bellevue and Shoreline Community College diving programs and deemed to have fulfilled the basic requirements for Project Sea-Use. In addition several hours of classroom and laboratory instruction preceded several days of practice dives conducted at Lake Crescent on Washington State's Olympic Peninsula. The exercises were greatly improved and far safer than techniques used on previous missions to the Cobb. And for the first time, diver-selectees were trained in the use of a shark cage. From Lake Crescent, the diving cadre was taken by Navy Tug to the open ocean waters off the Straits of Juan de Fuca, where they practiced operating in non-protected waters.

After nearly two months of intensive training and testing, the divers who qualified joined the scientist and engineers aboard the Coast Guard Cutter "Cactus" for the trip to Cobb.

Sea-Use lV-A resulted in the deployment of a lighted radar reflector buoy and inspection of the rock bolt anchors placed on the pinnacle in 1970. The main emphasis of the lV-A mission however was to study the physiology of open ocean diving. That is why there was so much attention given this time to the selection and training of divers. The Cobb itself provided the best and really only opportunity for training in open ocean SCUBA operations. With the last mission's shark encounters, the Sea-Use team this time brought with them a shark cage from which scientist might "study" any shark activity. There was none.

Because most of the dives on the Seamount required de-compression, there was always a decompression chamber as part of the on-board equipment and a qualified physician as part of the Sea-Use diving team, The bends, or the effects of nitrogen, without decompression was a real threat. As a matter of routine, divers were checked for nitrogen build up in their bodies using what was called the Doppler Bubble Detection method. Developed by Virginia Mason's Dr. Merrill Spencer and Diving Supervisor Campbell while in charge of The Virginia Mason Research Center in Seattle, the technique used sound to detect any bubbles in the blood stream. Any diver, in whom nitrogen bubbles were detected was restricted from repetitive decompression dives. Any more severe symptoms, like pain in the joints, would result in a "chamber ride" until the doc's were sure the diver was ok. Using this method proved quite successful, cutting the average cases of the "bends" from 5% to zero. It was for this reason that all dives on this mission were timed to fall well within the prescribed times for depth.

During one of the last dives of IV-A, team Doctor Don Callison had joined Campbell and Roland White for a tour of the chain link highway. It was more of an orientation for Doctor Callison. Even though he was a qualified SCUBA diver, he had spent all his time until now aboard ship tending to the medical needs of the crew and the divers. Campbell thought that while on the bottom it would be great idea for the three of them to gather up a bag full of the large succulent scallops that littered the pinnacle. After the tour of the chain link highway, the trio of divers began to scoop up the scallops and place them in a "lift" bag and send it to the surface. The "bag" was filled with compressed air in addition to the scallops and would rise to the surface on its own, guided only by a line held by the diver below. Above them the safety divers in the Zodiac would then empty the bag and send it back down. That was the plan! But much to the divers' surprise when the line played out the bag began to rise, only to stop and fall back to the pinnacle. Thinking it was too heavy, Campbell took out half the scallops and sent the bag back to the surface. All three divers, including Doctor Callison had by now two minutes to get to the decompression station suspended beneath the Zodiac. As the three began their ascent, the lift bag again floated gently past them headed for the pinnacle. Again, Campbell unloaded the bag, but this time noticed a one half inch tear in the bag. "No wonder." he though to himself. Meanwhile time was running out and if the divers didn't get to the decompression station they could get the bends. The seconds ticked by. The divers would have to forgo the luxury of scallops for dinner as they needed to get on with surviving the dive. At forty feet Campbell looked but couldn't find the decompression station. Panic was not part of Campbell's nature, but he couldn't speak for the other two, especially Dr. Callison. They were about 150 feet from the line that held the decompression air tank and the last thing any of them wanted to do was to surface without decompressing even though there was chamber aboard the ship. Fortunately the safety divers in the Zodiac spotted the diver's bubbles as they boiled to the surface and moved toward them. With barely a minute to go, Campbell looked up, saw the descending line. Air tanks were no longer attached to the line below the surface as in previous missions, instead breathing regulators were attached to long hoses attached to tanks in the Zodiac safety boats. Campbell motioned for his companions to head toward the line. They made it, with barely a half minute to spare…maybe less! Campbell was much relieved, especially that Doctor Callison was safe…some orientation dive, he thought to himself.

Marginal weather kept the number of dives on lV-A to less than forty, compared to more than 90 dives during Sea-Use lll. Never-the-less, Campbell and crew considered the mission a success, especially the training of the divers of whom he was very proud and said he would put them up against any diving team. Campbell noted that not only had his team become exceptional divers, but good seaman as well!

sea use V

Campbell was quick to call upon many of those same divers for Sea-Use V, the 1972 expedition to the Cobb Seamount. The Sea-Use V mission was funded by the US Maritime Administration which wanted to increase its body of knowledge of wave actions off the coast and above the mountain. In addition, Campbell hoped to re-orient the mooring anchors to better hold ships on station. The trip, he said, would also be an opportunity for additional diver training and studies in diving physiology.

This time operating from the deck of the Coast Guard Cutter "Iris" the divers managed to spend in excess of ten hours on the pinnacle and accomplished all tasks assigned.

One of those tasks was to take a series of photographs to be made into a mosaic that would provide a panorama of the pinnacle's Eastern flank. The job of taking the pictures fell to Bob McKee who, in addition to his normal diving gear carried with him two Nikonos Underwater Cameras. In order to take the pictures with one camera, Bob had to toss the other over his shoulder to his back. As he was shooting a very large rock-fish was swimming around him, more curious that dangerous, eying the camera on his back. Suddenly the huge fish dove toward Bob and snatched the camera from his back…strap and all. McKee, not knowing what had happened, found himself being dragged across the pinnacle by the large rock fish. McKee tried desperately to turn abound, but couldn't. After several yards, the fish let go and Bob floated free. Had it not been for his regulator mouthpiece, Campbell might have drowned, but knew laughing through a regulator mouthpiece could be dangerous.

Bob was ok and the camera…well, it would have to be a souvenir as it would never take pictures again.

During the next three years, The Sea-Use Council directed more trips to the Cobb Seamount, but unlike the missions of 1968, '69 and '70, the more recent expeditions reflected the new priorities of the Sea-Use program. In 1972 two trips to the Seamount resulted in the establishment of a wave height meter on the pinnacle. There were continued biological studies of the ocean area on and near the Seamount as well as additional diving physiology studies.

There were two more trips in 1973, one of which was to recover the wave height meter set on the summit the year before. The other trip was to provide support for acoustic studies being undertaken by the Navy Research Laboratory of ARPA. As before Spence Campbell was the diving supervisor on those trips, and as before he again drew on the ever growing list of open ocean divers he had trained, to make up the dive teams.

For the first time, data from the wave measuring instruments recovered from the Seamount dazzled scientists. It showed that several huge waves had swept the mountain top, some of them measuring over 120 feet high with enough force to sweep all but the most secure objects from the pinnacle. The data backed up the diver's contention that the mutilated instruments recovered during Sea-Use lll, were damaged by the wave action and not foreign trawlers as some had suggested.

The second of the two 1973 missions was aboard the USNS "Bartlett" an oceanographic research vessel assigned to the Military Sealift Command in Oakland, California. Making sure the "Bartlett" would stay on station was the a goal of the mission and divers were tasked with positioning the ship's anchor lines and securing it to the cemented bolts and shackles. Securing a vessel on the Cobb Seamount was essential to long term study of the mountain and the sea around it.

Just as important as the mooring of the Bartlett, was the deployment of a vary large and very expensive transducer to the East end of the pinnacle. It belonged to the US Navy and would be used to transmit low frequency sound signals to a receiving station in San Diego, California. Although the Navy wouldn't say, it was widely presumed that the transducer was to be used for communicating with US Submarines operating in the Pacific Ocean.

The two tasks were completed as planned with the only incident being the appearance of large schools of sharks showing up as divers were anchoring the transducer to the mountain top. Diving Supervisor Campbell said "at times there were as many as thirty to forty sharks." He noted further that in all his dives of the Cobb, he had never seen that many sharks at one time, especially at the depths the divers were working. Nor had he ever seen sharks deeper than sixty feet. Apparently the sharks were just curious and there were no incidents. The mission was pronounced a success.

The last two and final trips under the Project Sea-Use banner occurred in 1974 and '75…both for diver training.

As it turned out the 1974 mission was hardly routine as it marked the first time in the nearly ten years of Project Sea-Use, that women took an active part in the under-sea, open ocean operations. There was a nominal amount of "it's about time!" comments, but it had been Campbell's intent from the very beginning that only the best, most qualified divers, regardless of gender, would participate. There was no doubt, in Campbell's mind or the other divers for that matter, that Sharon Dodge and Sandy Orlich were qualified for Project Sea-Use. Dodge, in addition to being the board of the Diving Institute of Technology, was an advanced diving instructor and had been a member of an all-female aquanaut team that occupied an underwater habitat in the Virgin Islands. Ms. Orlich, a registered nurse was a qualified diver, and trained in submarine medicine. She was assigned to assist the team Doctor Bill Postles in his research in underwater medicine.

It had been long suspected by both scientists and divers, that the stress and anxiety of open ocean diving contributed to diving physiology, more specifically decompression sickness. It was Doctor Postles's intent to either prove or disprove the theory during this trip.

Before leaving for the Cobb, six divers, chosen by Dr. Postles, participated in a decompression chamber dive to a simulated 160 foot depth for ten minutes, which according to early US Navy Dive Tables, would require decompression. In the chamber test the participants were brought to the "surface" without decompression or stopping to allow the nitrogen bubbles to disburse. Not one of them demonstrated any decompression sickness as was expected. Doctor Postles then sought to test his theory that decompression sickness was in fact related somehow to the stress of open ocean diving. Diving Supervisor Campbell and diver Roland White went into the water and descended to 160 fleet where they remained for just over ten minutes. They used the time to collect scallops, again, and this time the lift bag worked. After the time had passed, Campbell and White headed for the surface and the waiting Zodiac but without stopping at ten feet below the surface as the decompression protocol required. The two were taken by the Zodiac to the ship and hoisted aboard. Neither of them exhibited any symptoms of decompression sickness. But as Campbell was getting out of his wet suit minutes later, he complained of some discomfort in his elbow. Doctor Postles checked Campbell out using the doppler system and determined the Campbell was experiencing stage three nitrogen bubble development. The pain in his elbow intensified and Campbell said it felt like someone injecting warm liquid metal into the joint. Wasting little time Postles ushered Campbell into the decompression chamber that was brought along for just such emergencies. Inside, both Campbell and Postles were taken to a depth of sixty feet, then brought back to the surface pressure, slowly so as to dissipate the nitrogen in his system. The treatment worked and the decompression time was drastically shortened.

But in what can be describe as one of those "whew, that was close," kind of moments, Campbell had no time to take off the bottom part of his wet suit. The problem was that his diving knife was still strapped to his leg with a day- night flare strapped to the knife. It presented a danger in the oxygen rich environment of the chamber and Campbell had visions of the entire chamber exploding into an orange ball of flame. He quickly signaled the operator to bring the chamber pressure to 30 feet and once the outer lock pressure equaled the inner lock pressure, Campbell opened the hatch and quickly handed the knife and flare to the technician outside. Once done, Campbell and Postles turned their attention to the "bends" which, because of the pressure in the chamber and the 100% oxygen had by now gone away.

On a second dive, the parameters of which were exactly the same as the dive Campbell and White had made, the two test divers experienced no decompression sickness what-so-ever. Not so however for the third set of divers. Upon returning to the surface, both complained of some nitrogen induced pain and were treated in the decompression chamber. In each case the treatments were successful and none of the divers experienced any residual effects.

Doctor Postles was delighted with the experiment and saw the results as supporting his theory that there is a relationship between decompression sickness and the the anxiety and physical stress of open ocean diving., noting the different divers will handle the physical stress differently.

After several more dives, the teams bundled up their gear and the ship headed for home. In was the last Sea-Use mission to Cobb Seamount.

EPILOG

Among its accomplishments, Project Sea-Use brought much appreciated attention to the State of Washington and the Pacific Northwest as a"mecca" for oceanography. Whether the program would result in establishing the State as a National Oceanographic Center, as the State Legislature postulated when it created the Oceanographic Commission, remained to be seen.

Many of the divers and scientists went back to their jobs, while some found other projects to occupy their time. It wasn't that they lost interest or the energy to continue their probe of the Cobb Seamount, it was a matter of money. The states, those private companies that participated and the Federal Government were frankly, unwilling to put any more money into a program that, while an adventure did not result in what they perceived as usable scientific accomplishments. It wasn't that the information gained from exploration of the Cobb Seamount was not valuable. To the contrary, it added a great deal to the fields of meteorology, oceanography, and navigation, to name three. But the more dramatic tasks, such as building a habitat on the pinnacle or providing "routine" visits to the Seamount with submersibles was financially too "rich" for the participants, and they had other things to do.

The Oceanographic Commission wasn't left holding an empty bag however. The organization returned to its original mandate which was to oversee the State of Washington's participation in any activities that had to do with the ocean's resources. And it appeared there was plenty to do. The Commission immediately "dived" into the field of aquaculture, fisheries and marine navigation and safety by sponsoring studies regarding their advisability and profitability. Of particular interest to the Commission, and certainly the Pacific Northwest as well was the transit of oil supertankers through the Puget Sound. Fears of shipping accidents and oil spills prompted study after study and ultimately led to legislation that regulated oil transport through areas of pristine waters. The Commission also extended its efforts to education, providing exhibits and speakers for local area high schools and colleges.

In 1980, five years after the end of Project Sea-Use, Doctor Dixy Lee Ray, a former chairperson of the Commission, now governor of the State of Washington, recommended that the Oceanographic Commission not be funded for the 1981-83 biennium. She argued that the Commission was not a regulatory body, nor did it produce any revenue, and it was not essential to the public's health and safety. There were many who disagreed stating that there remained a need for such a commission as there was no other State, Federal or private organization with the necessary authority and expertise to carry out the mandate. The Oceanographic Commission was unique in that regard, they said.

Apparently not unique enough however. By ceasing operations in June of 1981, The Oceanographic Commission all but ended any hope of returning to the Cobb Seamount.

No matter how well planned or how well prepared, no one, not even the Sea-Use Divers could have foreseen the problems encountered exploring the Seamount...but such is the way of exploring unknown worlds. The divers spent many uncomfortable hours probing the mysteries of the Seamount and many times returned with very little. But what they did learn each time was added to that which was learned before and in time a great deal of knowledge was gained.

Despite many hours of hard work, the Cobb Seamount as a scientific objective, became less important and gave way to more functional studies such as the environment. There was no single reason for this. Commander Charles Gott USN (ret) the Assistant Secretary of the Sea-Use Council stated;

"If Cobb Seamount became less of a priority, it was because of several things, not just one. While refusal of the National Science Foundation to fund the National Seamount Station proposal had some impact, so did the separation of the Sea Use Council and the

Oceanographic Institute of Washington...and the economy, which was by then beginning to force far thinking businessmen who had participated in the Sea-Use program not to think so far ahead as to outrun their financial responsibilities..."

But the divers, technicians and scientists should in no way think their efforts were for nothing. Far from it. Because of their dedication and boldness, new chapters were written in the annuls of open ocean diving. The work they accomplished on the Seamount contributed substantially to the art of ocean engineering. And the physiological, biological and geologic studies conducted at the Cobb added significantly to knowledge of the worlds oceans. Did the project set it sights too high? Maybe, but without any sights at all, Cobb Seamount would still be just a ten thousand foot high mountain rising from the ocean floor, the undisturbed home for those creatures that inhabit the sea. The Cobb Seamount has become, largely because of a change in Sea-Use priorities, a laboratory for the study of the environment. And who's to say that's not the way it should be. Certainly without the efforts of Project Sea-Use and its divers and scientists, Cobb Seamount wouldn't even serve that important function.

As anticipated there were, in the decades following Project Sea-Use, other assaults on Cobb Seamount. One of them, in 1973, was a mission whereby divers assisted in the placing of two acoustic monitors on the Seamount's pinnacle for the purpose of conducting long range sound propagation studies in the Pacific Ocean.

A far more extensive project was conducted in 2012 by a consortium of Fisheries and Oceans of Canada, NOAA, Environment Canada and several universities. The eleven day expedition used remotely operated underwater vehicles and divers to collect great amounts of scientific data on the flora and fauna of the Seamount and it's environment.

The reports generated from the 2012 expedition made little or no mention of evidence left on the pinnacle from the Project Sea-Use missions, although there was some interest noted in establishing some sort of platform on the pinnacle for the permanent installation of scientific observation.

In the future there will be other assaults on the Cobb, other attempts to put things on the pinnacle or to inhabit the mountain itself. And if they fall short? No matter, there will be others who, like the men and women of Project Sea-Use, share the belief that answers to our crowded land masses, our dwindling energy supplies and the growing need for food, can be found in the oceans that surround us

The US Fish & Wildlife Vessel John N. Cobb

During Sea-Use l, divers operated from the ESSA Research Ship Oceanographer using the ship's small boats. In the background the Oceanographer steams directly above the Seamount

Divers and safety divers man one of the Zodiac Boats that were use in subsequent operations on the Seamount. They proved to be more efficient and safer than larger boats.

Bottom Left: Crews prepare the explosive anchor that was launched during Sea-Use ll. Note the arrowhead-like flukes. **Bottom Right**: Divers Campbell and Eurick enter the ocean above the pinnacle using the collapsable diving stage.

This composite photograph shows Diving Supervisor Spence Campbell inspecting what remained of the Oregon State University Totem II instrument mast that was found on the summit during Sea-Use I. The upper portion of the mast was lost off the mountain and part of the mast visible in the picture was subsequently swept from the mountain top by strong currents.

Bottom Left: Divers Carl Eurick, John Patton and Roland White man the diving station aboard the Oceanographer during Sea-Use 1. From here pressure and air flow are regulated for the divers below. The large tank in front of the dive station is the decompression chamber. **Bottom Right:** A Diver-technician uses a ram-set tool to secure the Nerus Serge Meter to the mountain top

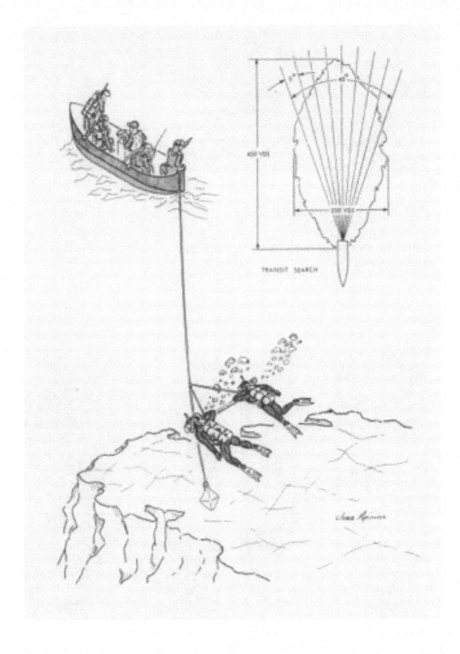

In an effort to make the best use of the diver's time on station and to cover as much area as possible, a technique called "riding anchor" was developed. As depicted in this sketch by diver Vince Rainier, two divers were towed across the pinnacle on a bar in a fan-like progression. The anchor below them allowed them to maintain a constant height above the pinnacle.

Following Sea-Use ll the divers and technicians embarked on an event that would hope-fully raise public and private awareness of Project Sea-Use. Utilizing a surplus net-buoy, the team created and occupied a habitat in Puget Sound. Top: The habitat being launched from Haines Wharf near Edmonds.

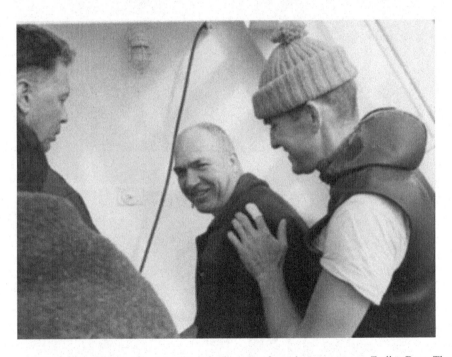

Top: Safety divers tend to two divers in the water from the ever-present Zodiac Boat. The three cylinders on the back of the diver on the right are buoyancy compositors which help balance the diver at any given depth.   **Bottom**: Diver Chuck Blackstock (on the right) gives a congratulatory pat-on-the-back to fellow diver Jim Gavin after he emerged from a marathon session in the decompression chamber after the near fatal mishap during Sea-Use l.

During the second of two Sea-Use missions in 1973, project divers placed a large transducer at the East end of the pinnacle. The transducer belonged to the US Navy and was to be used to "communicate" with a station in San Diego. Although the Navy wouldn't say, it was believed to have something to do with submarine traffic. **Top:** Technicians prepare to lower the transducer from the deck of the USNS Bartlett.

The 180 Foot Coast Guard Buoy Tender "Iris"

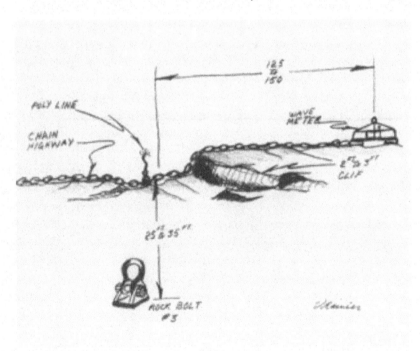

Diver-artist Vince Rainier's depiction of the chain link highway in the Cobb's summit. The sketch also show the location of the wave meter and the rock bolts that were used to assist in the mooring of ships.

Sea-Use diver guides one of the many instruments placed on the Cobb Seamount. It was standard practice for divers to assist in the lowering of all instruments and anchors to make sure they were placed and secured to a relatively flat surface.

Project Sea-Use Diving Supervisor Spence Campbell

the sea-use divers

Bill Aggenbach	Lelan Greff
Gary Peterson	George Axtell
Alan Hooke	Ken Poppenwell
Buddy Baer	Dick Jacoby
Vince Rainier	Dick Baldwin
Kirby Johnson	Mike Roberts
Chuck Birkeland	Dale Kisker
Mark Schaeffers	Chuck Blackstock
Ken Keintz	Jeff Scott
Steve Bottomiller	Mike Knowles
Robert Sheats	John Bain
Tom Landry	Edwin Smelzer
Ian Britt	LeRoy Lange
Neil Stainton	Donald Bloye
Dee Latham	Wayne Stockdale
Bill Brubaker	Buddy Lemus
Charles Stroeher	Warren Buck
Gregory LeVeque	Peter Taylor
Kevin Burke	James Lindsey
Jim Washburn	Spence Campbell

Bob Lium

Lyle Conner

Doug Wilson

Bob McKee

Kenneth Dodds

Roland White

Ron Mellin

John Erickson

Kent Smith

Jerry Niebuhr

Sandy Olrich

Dan Pace

Mike Patopeas

John Patton

Diane Parypa

John Williams

Al McCready

Donald Dodds

Wally White

Pat McKeown

Sharon Dodge

Keith Wood

Paul Morel

Carl Eurick

Lowell Forsman

Alan Francisco

Jim Gavin

Graham Gibbs

Al Gilmore

John Goode

sea-use scientist & technicians

Roderick Bliss	Ronald P. Hoss
Dr. Maurice Schwartz	Larry Liles
David Johnson	Eugene Smith
Keith Lingbloom	Dr. D.J. Jones
Robert Thurman	Louis Brown
Carol Mallo	John Williams
Sharon Dodge	Sandra Olrich
Spence Campbell	Brian Hamilton
Dr. David Pavear	Donald Handberg
Walter Sands	

oceanographic commission of washington

Donald Eldridge	Joe Mentor
Griffith Evans	Stan Murphy
George Farwell	John Murray
Slade Gorton	Dixy Lee Ray
John Hayden	John Ryder
George Johansen	Joe Stortini
Richard Kink	Don Talley

Glen Ledbetter

Brian Lewis

Jon Lindburgh

August Mardesich

Wesley Uhlman

Daniel Ward

Tal Watanabe

sea-use medical officers

Dr. Donald Callison

Dr. William Postles

Dr. Kent Smith

Dr. Leon Sealy

Dr. Merrill Spencer

the sea-use committee

Charles Blackstock

Bill Brubaker

Dr. Donald Callison

James Gavin

John Goode

Frank Henry

William High

Leiter Hockett

G.H. Lawther

Glenn Ledbetter

Edward Morgan

Dr. Leon Sealey

Robert Sheats

Dr. Peter Taylor

Peter Williams

Doug Wilson

project sea-use committees and support organizations

OCEANOGRAPHIC INSTITUTE OF WASHINGTON

Captain G. C. Evans Jr., Executive Director

Admiral E.D. Stanley Jr., Planning Director

Mr. Jon Lindberg, Special Consultant

BATELLE NORTHWEST LABS

Dr. William Kinsel, Mast Design Committee

UNIVERSITY OF WASHINGTON DEPT OF
OCEANOGRAPHY

Dr. L.H. Larsen, Mast Instrumentation Committee

Walter Sands, Site Survey Committee

Dr. Peter Taylor, Biological Investigations Committee

UNIVERSITY OF WASHINGTON MARINE
RESOURCES

Dr. Stanley Murphy, Acoustics Committee
Mr. John Dermody

UNIVERSITY OF ALASKA

Dr. Donald W. Hood

OREGON STATE UNIVERSITY

Dr. John Byrne

VIRGINIA MASON RESEARCH CENTER

Dr. Merrill Spencer, Diving Operations Committee

NORTHWEST DIVING INSTITUTE

Spence Campbell

GLOSSARY

ARPA

Advanced Research Projects Agency, An agency of the
United States Department of Defense. ARPA's name
was changed to Defense Advanced Research Projects
Agency (DARPA) in 1971.

ESSA

The U. S. Environmental Science Services Administration
(ESSA) was a United States Federal executive agency
created in 1965 as part of a reorganization of the United
States Department of Commerce (USDOC). Its
mission was to oversee the nation's weather and climate operations. In 1970 ESSA became the National
Oceanic and Atmospheric Administration. (NOAA)

BLUE SHARK

A species of shark that inhabits deep waters in the world's
temperate and tropical oceans. Preferring cooler waters
blue sharks migrate long distances. Generally lethargic,
Blue Sharks feed primarily on small fish and squid.

FATHOM

A unit of length equal to six feet (approximately 1.8 m), chiefly used in reference to the depth of water.

GREAT WHITE SHARK

A species of large shark in the coastal surface waters of all the major oceans. The great white shark is mainly known for its size up to 26 feet) in length and 7000 pounds.The great white shark is arguably the world's largest known predatory fish, and is ranked first in having the most recorded attacks on humans.

HYPERBARIC

A scientific term referring to producing pressures higher than that of normal atmosphere. This is usually accomplished in a Hyperbaric Chamber often used in div ing to treat decompression sickness or the bends by gradu- ally regulating pressure in order to reduce nitrogen bubbles in the diver's joints.

LORAN

Long Range Radio Navigation, a radio navigation system developed in the United States during World War II. It is operated at lower frequencies in order to provide improved range up to 1,500 miles (2,400 km) with accuracy of tens of miles.

MARITIME ADMINISTRATION

The United States Maritime Administration (MARAD) is an agency of the United States Department of Transportation. Its programs promote the use of waterborne transportation and its seamless integration with other segments of the transportation system, and promote the viability of the U.S. merchant marine.

MIXED GAS

Activity in which the diver breathes a mixture other than air. The main incentive to dive with "non-air" gas mixtures is to avoid nitrogen narcosis.

BANG STICK

A specialized firearm used underwater that is fired when in direct contact with the target. Power heads are often used for spear fishing and against sharks or alligators, for sport, defense, or to kill nuisance animals. The term powerhead refers to the firearm-like part of the device; when attached to a shaft.

NAVAL CIVIL ENGINEERING

The Civil Engineer Corps (CEC) is responsible for executing and managing the planning, design, acquisition, construction, operation, and maintenance of the Navy's shore facilities.

PONY BOTTLE

A pony bottle is a smaller air tank, which is carried in addition to the main tank. It possesses its own regulator with first and second stage and sometimes a separate pressure gauge.

PURSE SEINER

A fishing vessel that employs a seine , a fishing net that hangs vertically in the water with its bottom edge held down by weights and its top edge buoyed by floats.

RAMSET TOOL

A nail gun used in construction and manufacturing to join materials to hard substrates such as steel and concrete.The power is often provided by a charge such as a 22 calibre cartridge.

SATURATION DIVING

A diving technique that allows divers to reduce the risk of decompression sickness ("the bends") when they work at great depths for long periods of time.

SEALAB

Experimental underwater habitats developed by the United States Navy in the 1960s to prove the viability of saturation diving and humans living in isolation for extended periods of time.

SEA STATE

A sea state is the general condition of the surface on a large body of water and is characterized by wave height, wind and swells.

SCUBA

Self Contained Underwater Breathing Apparatus invented by Jaques Cousteau in 1943

SHARK BILLY

A club often carried by divers to fend off sharks or other underwater pests. Usually two to three feet long and sometimes equipped with a spike at one end.

TRAWLER

A fishing trawler, also known as a dragger, is a commercial fishing vessel designed to operate fishing trawls. Trawls are fishing nets that are pulled along the bottom of the sea or in midwater at a specified depth.

TROLLER

A fishing vessel where one or more fishing lines, baited with lures or bait fish, are drawn through the water.

USCGS

United States Coast and Geodetic Survey (USCGS), a United States federal agency that defines and manages a national coordinate system, providing the foundation for transportation and communication; mapping and charting; and a large number of applications of science and engineering. Since its foundation in its present form in 1970, it has been part of the National Oceanic and Atmospheric Administration (NOAA), of the United States Department of Commerce.

USNS

United States Naval Ships are auxiliary support vessels owned by the U.S. Navy and operated by Military Sealift Command. They are crewed by civilian mariners rather than U.S. Navy personnel.

WHITE TIP SHARK

A large pelagic shark inhabiting tropical and warm temperate seas. Its stocky body is most notable for its long, white-tipped, rounded fins. Described as dangerous and aggressive, this slow-moving fish dominates feeding frenzies, and is a danger to shipwreck or air crash survivors.

ZODIAC BOAT

A small boat characterized by a rigid floor suspended between two inflated rubber pontoons. Ideal for conditions often encountered in the open ocean. The name Zodiac is derived from the name of the company that developed the boat but has become the generic name for all boats of this design.

BIBLIOGRAPHY

books & periodicals

Archabold, Mike;   "Aquanauts Blaze Trail In Sea
Frontier" The Daily Astorian, Monday, July 8,1974

Birkeland, Chuck;   "Marine Life on Cobb Seamount"
Pacific Northwest Sea, OCW Vol 2 No 4 1969

Brubaker, Bill; " Sea Equipment Damaged" The
Everett Herald/Herald NewsService May 27, 1970

Budinger, Thomas; Cobb Seamount Deep Sea
Research Abstract, Vol. 14 Pergamon Press Ltd,
London, 1967

Battelle Memorial Institute & Honeywell Inc., Project
Sea Use, Proposed   Exploration of the Cobb
Seamount. The Oceanographic Commission of
Washington. Seattle 1969

Campbell, Spence; Lewis And Clark And Me,
Gorham Printing, Rochester, WA 2006

Department of The Navy; "Conquest Of Inner Space, the US Navy Sea-Lab lll   Experiment," Office of Naval Research Washington D.C. 1968

Diving Operations Report; Project Sea-Use lV September 8, 1971

Ellison, J.G.; "Exploratory Fishing Vessel John N. Cobb" Fishing leaflet 385, U.S. Department of Interior, Washington D.C. October 1950

Hayden, John: Chairman of the Washington Oceanographic Commission "Report to the Legislature", January 1969

Hoss, Ronald; "Diving to a Mountain Top" The Seattle Times, November 9, 1969

Ledbetter, B.G.; "Seamounts-Name Dropping Along The Pacific Northwest Coast" Pacific Northwest Sea OCW   Seattle, 1969

Log Book of the John N. Cobb, June 12, 1950 to September 16, 1950 University of Washington, Seattle

Log Book of the USCGC Ivy (WLB-329) August 19-29, 1969

Log Book of the MV Brown Bear, University of Washington, Cruise #364, May 21 to June 3, 1965

Man In The Sea Program, fact sheet, U.S. Navy Deep Submergence Systems Project, Washington D.C.

McManus, Dean A; Physiography Of Cobb and Gorda Rises, Northeast Pacific Ocean, Abstract Geological Society of America 1967

Oceanographic Commission of Washington State; Operations Guide for Project Sea Use, Seattle, September 20, 1968

Oceanographic Institute of Washington; "Task Development for the Sea Use Program, " 1st Edition, Seattle, WA. March 1, 1969

O'Neal, H.A; Project Sea-Lab 1 Summary Report, Office of Naval Research, Department of the Navy, Washington D.C. 1965

Pacific Northwest Sea; "Anchor Bolts On Cobb" Fall 1970 Vol. 3 No. 3 Oceanographic Commission of Washington, Seattle, WA.

Page, Don; "Probe of Oceans Begins On Friday" Seattle Post Intelligencer, Seattle, WA. October 2,1968

Page, Don; "Sea Sickness on a Mountain," Seattle Post Intelligencer, Seattle, WA Wednesday September 3, 1969

Page, Don; "Divers Plan 3-Day Study Under The Sea," Seattle Post Intelligencer, Seattle WA. Tuesday April 21,1969

Page, Don; "Divers Fail To Find Seamount Devices," Seattle Post Intelligencer, May 23, 1970

Page, Don; "Study To Measure Ocean Waves," Seattle Post Intelligencer, Saturday August 1971

Pauli , D.C. & Clapper, G.P. Project Sea-Lab ll Summary Report, Office of Naval Research, Department of the Navy, Washington D.C. 1967

Prueter, A.T; "Seattle Exploratory Dishing And Gear Research Base," National Marine Fisheries Research Center, Seattle, October 6, 1970

Seattle Post Intelligencer; "1st Photos from Cobb Seamount." Thursday October 10, 1968

Seattle Post Intelligencer; "Sound Floor Object of Cozy Search," Monday, November 3, 1969

Seattle Times;"Divers Begin Seamount Project" April 26, 1970

Sheats, Robert; Personal Diary, USCGC "Ivy" Project Sea Use ll

Sterr, Glenn; "1969 Cobb Seamount Expedition a Success," Seattle Times, Wednesday September 3, 1969

Spencer, Merrill MD; Medical Report On Project Sea-Use 1, Virginia Mason Research Center, Seattle, WA 1968

Spencer, Merrill MD; Campbell, S.D.; Eurick, C.V; "Diving to Cobb Seamount" Journal Of Occupational Medicine ll-5 pp 285-291 May 1969

Technical Report # 60; " Cobb Seamount, A Deep Sea Feature off the Washington Coast," Department of Oceanography, University of Washington, Seattle 1960

USCGS Oceanographer-OSS 01; U.S. Department of Commerce, Environmental Science Services Administration, U.S. Government Printing Office, Washington D.C;

Washington State Substitute House Bill 762; "Commissions, Board, Councils-Abolishment, Transfer of Powers, Section 20," Washington State Legislature, Olympia WA., 1982

White, Wallace; "Anchor Bolts Cemented Into Cobb," Pacific Northwest Sea Vol. 3 No. 3 Seattle, WA 1970

Williams, Hill; "Ocean Project Is Tough Job," Seattle Times, Thursday October 10, 1968

William, Hill; Submarine Laboratory Urged on Pacific Seamount," Seattle Times, Sunday, December 14, 1969

Williams, Hill; "Seamount Could Become Unusual Open Air Laboratory," Seattle Times, Seattle WA. 1970

Williams, Hill; "Cobb Seamount: Short on Funds, Long on Potential," Seattle Times, October 18, 1970

Williams, Hill; "Cobb Seamount Instruments Recovered in Damaged State," Seattle Times 1970

interviews

Dr. Robert Burns

Spencer Campbell

J.G. Ellison

Griffith Evans

Carl Eurick

Charles Gott

Ronald Hoss

Sheldon Johnson

B.G. Ledbetter

Jon Lindbergh

Stanley Murphy

Don Page

Vince Rainier

Jim Washburn

Roland White

Hill Williams

Walter Sands

Dr. Merrill Spencer

letters

Campbell, Spencer, Chairman of the Sea Use Diving Committee to Bill Brubaker, February 19, 1969

Codiga, Daniel; University Of Washington, Department of Oceanography to Bill Brubaker, March 8, 1983

Spencer, Merrill MD; Project Sea Use Medical Director to Bill Brubaker, March 18, 1969

Washburn, James; Department of Oceanographer, Oregon State University to Bill Brubaker, April 23, 1972

press releases

Boeing News Service; "Boeing Successfully
Demonstrates Meteor Burst Communication," Seattle,
June 14, 1964

Oceanographic Commission of Washington;
"Deepstar To Explore Cobb Seamount, Seattle,
January 22,1969

Oceanographic Commission of Washington; "Sea Use
Program a Success,: Seattle, September 2,1969

Sea-Use Council of Washington; "1st Trip to Cobb."
Seattle May 29, 1973

University Of Washington News Service, Seattle 1965

"We need people to understand the sea and be involved in it...not just a few people, but all of us. Let's go to sea to stay and make the sea productive through our American ingenuity!"

Athelstan Spilhaus
Oceanographer

ABOUT THE AUTHOR

While a long time Seattle broadcast journalist, Bill Brubaker often specialized in reporting on stories relating to diving and marine research. He produced several television documentaries on the subject. He served on the Sea-Use Committee and as a Project Sea-Use historian. This is his first book on this subject. He is the author of a book about television news entitled *Never As It Seems*, and was a contributing editor/writer of the book *Wings At The Ready, a history of the US Naval Air Reserve.*

Bill lives with his wife Marlene in Edmonds, Washington